INDEPENDENT
THINKING
ON ...

MFL

Crista Hazell

HOW TO MAKE MODERN FOREIGN LANGUAGE TEACHING
EXCITING, INCLUSIVE AND RELEVANT

independent
thinking press

First published by

Independent Thinking Press
Crown Buildings, Bancyfelin, Carmarthen, Wales, SA33 5ND, UK
www.independentthinkingpress.com

and

Independent Thinking Press
PO Box 2223, Williston, VT 05495, USA
www.crownhousepublishing.com

Independent Thinking Press is an imprint of
Crown House Publishing Ltd.

Page 16, top figure: from Tinsley, T. and Board, K. (2013) *Languages for the Future: Which
Languages the UK Needs Most and Why* (London: British Council). Available at: https://www.
britishcouncil.org/sites/default/files/languages-for-the-future-report.pdf. © British Council, 2013.
Used with permission. Page 16, bottom figure: from https://internetworldstats.com/stats7.htm ©
Miniwatts Marketing Group, 2017. Used with permission. Pages 56–57: pose, pause, pounce,
bounce © Pupils First UK Ltd. Created by Pam Fearnley (pamb566@btinternet.com). Pages
138–142: GCSE personal preparation game plan used with kind permission of Andy Philip Day.

Quotes from Ofsted and Department for Education documents used in this
publication have been approved under an Open Government Licence. Please see:
http://www.nationalarchives.gov.uk/doc/open-government-licence/version/3/.

Edited by Ian Gilbert.

The Independent Thinking On ... series is typeset in Azote, Buckwheat TC Sans,
Cormorant Garamond and Montserrat.

The Independent Thinking On ... series cover style was designed by Tania Willis
www.taniawillis.com.

British Library Cataloguing-in-Publication Data
A catalogue entry for this book is available from the British Library.

Print ISBN 978-178135337-0
Mobi ISBN 978-178135357-8
ePub ISBN 978-178135358-5
ePDF ISBN 978-178135359-2

LCCN 2019956614

Printed and bound in the UK by
Gomer Press, Llandysul, Ceredigion

FOREWORD

Since establishing Independent Thinking in 1994, we have worked hard to share with educators around the world our belief that there is always another way. The Independent Thinking On ... series of books is an extension of that work, giving a space for great educators to use their words and share great practice across a number of critical and relevant areas of education.

Independent Thinking on MFL is a book that couldn't have come at a better time. As I write these words, it's 2020 and the world is splintering in a way it hasn't done so for decades. Politicians around the globe are stoking nationalism and isolationism in a way that pits 'us' against 'them' and makes political currency out of vilifying anyone who is 'other'. If all you know is your type, your culture, people who look and speak like you, then this is quite an easy thing to do.

But what happens when you have a world view that embraces other perspectives? When you spend time learning about 'them' and immersing yourself in their culture? When you are able to communicate directly in the language of the 'other'?

What happens is that you realise there is no other.

As a former MFL teacher myself, I know the power that learning languages has to transform our views of the world. While the school syllabus can get bogged down in buying cabbages and asking your way to the *quincaillerie*, the best language teachers see a greater purpose for their work, one that involves helping their students to find their place in a bigger world.

And talking of the best language teachers, there is no better person to write this book than Independent Thinking Associate Crista Hazell. With many years' experience as a successful MFL teacher and head of languages, Crista shares so many great insights, approaches and ideas that will transform language teaching in any primary or secondary classroom.

If we want the world to come back together, where else to start but in talking together, whatever the language.

IAN GILBERT
YORK

ACKNOWLEDGEMENTS

To the wonderful men in my life who have inspired, supported, encouraged and loved me – Dad, Jon and the zoo. Thank you for everything, especially your never-ending patience, smiles and support.

This book would not have been possible without the love, support, patience and kindness of many people, including Ian Gilbert, Nina Jackson and the Independent Thinking family.

Thank you to Emma Tuck for her patience and support and to the wonderful people at the Independent Thinking Press collective for their tireless encouragement.

Thank you also to the many people who have known me, helped me, supported me and inspired me on this journey – you know who you are.

CONTENTS

FIRST THOUGHTS

Firstly, thank you for purchasing *Independent Thinking on MFL*, which is one of a series of titles from Independent Thinking Press. Check out the other titles too – they are definitely worth adding to the continuing professional development (CPD) library in your department or school. If you don't have one yet, then what an excellent way to start!

This book is for MFL teachers of all ages and stages – those who are new to the profession and those with more experience – written by an experienced MFL teacher who thinks that being a teacher is the best job in the world. It has been inspired by my adventures in the classroom over 20 years. I am grateful to the wonderful young people I have had the privilege of teaching: they have challenged and inspired me, and I hope I have returned the favour. It is heartening to have witnessed the way so many learners have battled through the key stages and become brilliant linguists, who now use their language knowledge and skills in their daily lives working as engineers, doctors, artists, photographers, midwives, zookeepers and shopkeepers. There are also learners who have been inspired and moved by the culture and traditions beyond this green and pleasant land who have gone on to travel far and wide on exotic adventures. Finally, there are who that have become teachers who are promoting languages in their daily work. I am very proud of them all.

For trainees, newly qualified teachers (NQTs) and recently qualified teachers (RQTs): This book should serve to support you in your learning journey to becoming a marvellous MFL teacher. It includes tips, strategies, methods and activities, all of which I have successfully used in the classroom with learners from Key Stage 2 to Key Stage 5. There is also a specific help section in Chapter 10. My advice on where to start is to know your learners really well, beyond any data. If you build the relationship first, the language learning will come.

For experienced MFL teachers: I am amazed by the collegiality and positivity of MFL teachers and the MFLTwitterati, and the colleagues I have met at TeachMeets, conferences and languages events – thank you for your smiles and support. I hope you enjoy using this book to enhance the MFL experience in your classrooms.

For teachers who are not based in England: I do make reference to features of the education system in England, as this is what has framed my practice. Key stages are obviously not universal terminology, but I hope that you will understand what I mean and equate this to the system in which you work. For guidance, learners are aged 7–11 in Key Stage 2; 11–14 in Key Stage 3; 14–16 in Key Stage 4 (at the end of which GCSEs are sat); and 16–18 in Key Stage 5 (at the end of which they take their A levels).

For overseas colleagues: I hope you find the following pages helpful and insightful for integrating into your practice with second-language learners. Or for those of you in international schools who want to mix up your teaching style to support ex-pats, or indeed the local children and young people with whom you work, there is plenty here for you to choose from. Enjoy the journey!

CHAPTER 1

HOOK THEM INTO LEARNING

One of the learning hooks that I enjoy using in the MFL classroom is asking the question, 'What is your favourite foreign language word?' I also ask this question in workshop sessions and at conferences. I love seeing people's faces as they trawl through their vast philological memory, deftly sifting through all the languages they have learned and selecting one single word. Whether they are teachers, school leaders, teaching assistants (TAs), foreign language assistants (FLAs) or students, their expressions fascinate me. The visible excitement as their brains locate their favourite word is fantastic, although inevitably there is also some conflict in the choice of which word takes the top spot. At this point I add that they can have one word per language, and their anxiety fades and their eyes begin to sparkle. The pleasure individuals show as they share their special words is a joy to behold. Often, the words are well-loved with others in the room; there is nodding, grinning and the positivity spreads like wildfire. It's wonderful to see.

The emotional connection to a particular word often returns the speaker to a special happy place, perhaps in the classroom, a memory from childhood or an international experience with friends, teachers or peers. When I ask why a word is so beloved, people frequently say that they like the way it sounds, the way it rolls off the tongue, the way it makes them smile or laugh as they enunciate it, the quirkiness of the word, the mix of graphemes and phonemes,[1] or simply because it's such a beautiful word. Regardless of the reason, it always seems to make folk feel happy. These words create a ripple of smiles, like a Mexican wave, moving across the room and creating an excited buzz.

Emotional connectivity to strange and interesting words linked to powerful memories can be harnessed to develop vocabulary range and depth, sentence structure and complexity in spoken and written work. It provides opportunities for pronunciation practice as well as the recall of interesting vocabulary. Below is a small selection of wonderful words which have been generously shared with me over the years – a fabulous philological flaunt-tant that has caused a fillyloo but always much glee!

A strategy for using wondrous target language words with students is to construct a 'best sentence' containing as many as possible. They should identify the gender and its

---

1   A phoneme is the smallest unit of sound in speech and a grapheme is a letter (or series of letters) that represent the sounds in speech.

placement, tackle tenses, negotiate negatives and place object pronouns in the construction. Students can use their creativity to generate fantastically original sentences, which has the effect of deepening the learning experience, not to mention wowing their peers. Students have to be aware of unfamiliar vocabulary in terminal assessments, so venturing off-piste in tasks like this, which forces them to identify and use unusual words, extends their expertise in this area. Best sentences can also be used as a dictation or storytelling activity; speaking tasks create additional opportunities to develop oracy skills. There are lots of options.

I remember my first ever French lesson: I loved learning this amazing new language which is spoken in France, Africa and beyond. It was at this point that I realised I could travel the world and communicate with other people in another language. I was at a middle school in Leeds, dressed in a brown and gold uniform, and in that instant my world changed forever. I ran home at the end of the day and proudly announced that I was going to be a French teacher. Some 14 years later I was graduating from Manchester Metropolitan University with a bachelor of education degree. The lass from Leeds was leaving to start a new life as a teacher, and it was the best feeling in the world – as it still is now. I had made it: I was realising my dream.

I'm not sure that my MFL teachers were aware of how much I adored their lessons (I would invariably complete my MFL homework first, often spending many hours on it) or how desperately I aspired to be a teacher, envisaging myself helping students like me to love languages, to be excited by languages and to travel the world using languages to communicate. It was that ability to converse with other people from across the globe in their native tongue that excited me most. It is such a joy to be able to teach others to make themselves understood in the markets of Marrakech, the terraces of Tunis, the cafés of Caen, the librairies of Lille, on public transport in Paris or asking questions in Quimper and Quebec. Moreover, language skills are needed in the UK to support business, trade, technology, finance, government, tourism, the NHS and our local communities. You name the career choice, and I'm certain that the ability to speak an additional language is an asset.

However, language learning in schools is in crisis because not enough time is being allocated to the subject. Languages are disappearing from school timetables amid the continuing pressure to keep budgets down. The decrease in the number of linguists at Key Stage 5 and the number who go on to study a language at university has resulted in the teaching profession recruiting native speakers from overseas to meet demand for languages teachers in UK schools. With additional constraints on our European partners following recent political decisions, the challenges are only set to increase. As well as teachers' contact time being increased, some teachers are also being asked to learn a new language over the summer to plug gaps in the timetable (despite already being able to speak three other languages fluently). I'm all for creative solutions but learning a new language in six weeks isn't valuing the subject, the teachers or the students.

The students I have taught haven't always seen how languages could help them in their careers, yet I know of former students with an eclectic mix of careers, all of whom have been called on to use their language skills with no notice and limited time to prepare. I was once on a British Airways flight preparing to enjoy some serious downtime in the sun. Midway into the journey, as others around me slept, I was awoken by several flight attendants with serious expressions. A passenger was seriously unwell and required medical attention, but the flight staff couldn't communicate with her. They didn't know whether the pilot needed to divert the plane to the next available airport or continue on to the destination.

It was my job to ascertain if the poorly and distressed passenger had a diagnosed medical condition. We established a language in common and, calmly but with a sense of urgency, I was directed to identify key information and details so the medically trained flight staff could intervene to relieve her symptoms and find out if the plane would have to land at the earliest opportunity. Despite serious breathing issues the passenger passed on the vital details. It was a tense time: the information I was communicating to flight staff needed to be precise. The role of translator had never particularly excited me; it was the ability to communicate with others, to speak and understand in the moment, that had spurred me on to learn languages at school. Yet there I was assisting a medical team with a seriously ill patient. I have always said to learners in my classroom that they don't know when they will need to use their language skills.

Former students have contacted me over the years to tell me how – while at work, on holiday or simply in the right situation at the right time – they have been called on to use their language skills to assist in an important or lifesaving situation. We know that having an additional language on top of your native tongue opens doors, so it's our job as MFL teachers to make sure that we prepare our students to be effective and tolerant communicators in their local communities and able to work with colleagues in other countries across the globe. We are a small island, so it is essential that we communicate and collaborate with our neighbours. We shouldn't expect everyone to speak our native tongue and so not attempt to learn other languages. The more we learn about other languages, the more we learn about other cultures. As global trade networks and markets develop, and digital technologies bring us ever closer together, the least we can do is learn to communicate effectively with our colleagues and partners worldwide.

When I've canvassed colleagues about what they enjoy about being MFL teachers, the sorts of responses I've received describe how they like that they could:

- Teach students to communicate in another language.

- Educate students about their first language through learning another language.

- Open students' hearts and minds to a life beyond their current home, village, town, city and country.

- Share with learners a skill they will have for life.

- Empower others to discover and make new, interesting sounds.

- Invite learners to discover novel, intriguing yet familiar words.

- Encourage international travel.

- Inspire thinking at a global level.

- Promote internationalism.

- Foster acceptance, understanding and tolerance of other people, cultures, customs, religions and traditions.

- Take students overseas to discover new lands, ideas, sounds and spaces.

- Train students to listen for gist as well as specific information.

- Support students to become excellent orators.

- Help students to make grapheme and phoneme links.

- Develop students' language confidence and fluency.

- Share a passion for languages.

- Give the gift of language learning to others.

- Help students to access a range of literature, music, drama, poetry and film in other languages.

- Support anxious learners to overcome their fear of making errors.

- Promote the concept that international borders aren't limits.

- Guide learners on a linguistic adventure.

- Embolden learners to become translators.

- Inspire a new generation of linguists and language learners.

- Give learners a skill that can be useful in every type of job and career.

- Open the door to learning additional languages.

- Empower learners by helping them to find and use their voices.

- Facilitate learners to access reading and listening materials in other languages on the internet and in print.

- Inspire learners by collecting 1,001 things from overseas holidays and visits to use in the classroom.

- Intrigue learners by recycling stories, articles and magazines, and gifting them to learners to read and be further inspired.

- Connect with other professionals and always be enthused by something new we have learned.

- Get paid for doing something we love!

In the rest of the book, I will share my thoughts, experiences and ideas on listening, speaking, reading and writing in the MFL classroom. All of these creative strategies have been used successfully by myself and other colleagues with learners of MFL and English as an additional language from Year 6 through to Year 13 – as well as with international students – to make language lessons exciting, inclusive and relevant. The chapters take you on a journey and provide an insight into what is possible.

There is no one way to teach languages – there are many different techniques. I am grateful to have found some novel ways to help learners access, engage with and become confident in language learning. I am also thankful for the openness, collegiality and collaboration of my colleagues, which has ensured the best possible language learning experiences for our MFL students.

CHAPTER 2

WELCOME THEM WITH A ПРИВЕТ

SHAPING LEARNERS OF ALL KINDS

Although some might regard it as controversial, I believe that everyone should be given the opportunity to learn an international language,[1] regardless of age, stage, ability, prior attainment, school or status. Many schools include all their students in language lessons, but some withdraw students for booster sessions of core subjects, thus limiting the breadth of curriculum provision. Teaching languages promotes the recognition of other languages, cultures and traditions – all of which students may encounter in school, in their local community or online – thereby promoting tolerance, appreciation and understanding. It is a feature of the statutory programmes of study,[2] and is therefore expected in every educational establishment in England.

Schools that know their students well, particularly those with cohorts with a diverse range of home and heritage

---

1 In line with the terminology used in the Curriculum for Wales 2022, I prefer to use the term international language, second language or MFL, rather than foreign language.

2 See https://www.gov.uk/government/publications/national-curriculum-in-england-framework-for-key-stages-1-to-4.

languages,[3] can make effective provision to support students who require it until they can access the curriculum independently. With exam systems operating almost entirely in English, heritage languages are not always openly embraced by schools, and the opportunity to engage young people in learning other languages is missed. This is a shame, and almost certainly a missed opportunity to enrich young people's knowledge and understanding of other cultures. The teaching of 'British values' is driven by the idea of acceptance, tolerance and mutual respect.[4] Learning a language within school is one way to ensure that these principles are assured and endorsed by all, as well as having the benefit of equipping students with the ability to understand their place in a culturally diverse society. It is the opportunities we get to experience that help us to learn, connect and become a community; embracing difference and diversity within the school community helps to build strong external communities.

Schools shape learners of all kinds, with aspirations and futures of their own design, for amazing adventures which we cannot predict or even fathom because they are yet to be created. Think of the technological age in which we are now living: did the teachers and school leaders in the

---

3   A heritage language is a language that children speak at home with their families. It may not be fully developed across all four language skills because of limited environmental input; however, every young person who interacts in a heritage language must be fully supported.

4   In 2014 the Department for Education stated that all schools in the UK had to promote British values. The five values are: democracy, the rule of law, individual liberty, mutual respect, and tolerance of those with different faiths and beliefs and those without faith. Although explicitly taught, it is expected that every school will have an ethos and climate which promotes British values. See Department for Education, *Promoting Fundamental British Values as Part of SMSC on Schools: Departmental Advice for Maintained Schools* (27 November 2014). Ref: DFE-00679-2014. Available at: https://www.gov.uk/government/publications/promoting-fundamental-british-values-through-smsc.

closing decades of the 20th century conceive of everything that is now possible? Our experiences to date serve only to provide perspectives on what has gone before, but the fact is that we are preparing learners for life in a new digital and technological century. Fellow school leavers from the local community are no longer the only competition; there are now potentially billions of competitors in the job market. If technology has made the world smaller, it is also full of incredible experiences for those who wish to participate. Since the launch of the International Space Station there has been only one UK visitor (Tim Peake) out of the 227 visitors from 19 countries. English is not the most commonly used language among the research team of astronauts orbiting Earth, so there are amazing opportunities for polyglot scientists.

According to the 2017 *Languages for the Future* study, the top ten most important languages for English speakers to learn are based on indicators which include:

- Current UK exports.

- The language needs of UK business.

- Future trade priorities.

- Emerging high growth markets.

- Diplomatic and security priorities.

- The public's language interests.

- Outward and inward tourism.

- International educational engagement.

- Levels of English proficiency in other countries.

● The prevalence of different languages on the internet.[5]

All of the above indicators are carefully considered, although Brexit may well mean that the landscape changes over the coming years in line with forthcoming trade agreements. However, the fact remains that the ten most important languages for the UK have remained the same since 2013:

1   Spanish

2   Mandarin Chinese

3   French

4   Arabic

5   German

6   Italian

7   Dutch

8   Portuguese

9   Japanese

10 Russian[6]

MFL is accessible for all, but only if the appropriate support is in place for the subject. MFL matters, so it is frustrating to hear of its disappearance from school curriculums, both at primary and secondary level. MFL deserves more than a few celebration days (European Day of Languages, Bastille Day, El Día de los Muertos, Christmas, Easter, New Year, etc.), half an hour here or there, or one two-hour block per

---

5   T. Tinsley and K. Board, *Languages for the Future: The Foreign Languages the United Kingdom Needs to Become a Truly Global Nation* (London: British Council, 2017), p. 4. Available at: https://www.britishcouncil.org/sites/default/files/languages_for_the_future_2017.pdf.

6   Tinsley and Board, *Languages for the Future*, p. 4. This can be compared to the 2013 report: T. Tinsley and K. Board, *Languages for the Future: Which Languages the UK Needs Most and Why* (London: British Council, 2013). Available at: https://www.britishcouncil.org/sites/default/files/languages-for-the-future-report.pdf.

week. If we are to meet the demands of teaching people to speak the languages required to keep the UK functioning with its European neighbours and international business and diplomatic partnerships, we need to ensure that young people's language learning experience is robust, engaging and widespread across all primary and secondary schools, and aim at all learners, not just the more 'academic'.

One argument against learning languages that is frequently put to me by students is that the internet is predominantly in English, and that, with technology ever more present in our lives, apps will instantaneously translate from one language to another, enabling us to become multilingual with just a single earpiece. According to this way of thinking, knowledge of other languages is unnecessary; however, for the foreseeable future this is simply untrue (see the figures below). In response, I suggest that although they can access only English websites at the moment, in time and with persistence they will be able to read French, German or Spanish sites, depending on the language they choose to study, which will make them more marketable. Reliable simultaneous translation is still a way off, so learning languages is still very much needed and should be encouraged. You can imagine the looks I receive!

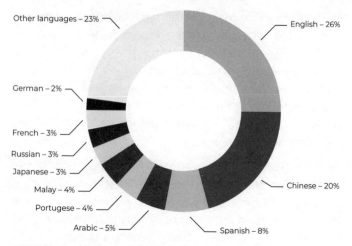

INTERNET USE BY LANGUAGE

Source: Tinsley and Board, *Languages for the Future* (2013), p. 16.

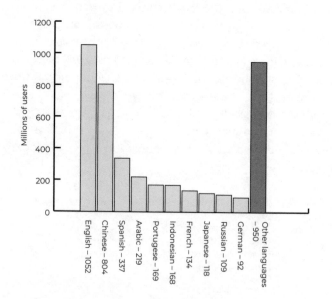

TOP TEN LANGUAGES ON THE INTERNET.
ESTIMATED TOTAL INTERNET USERS ARE 4,156,932,140
ON 31 DECEMBER 2017

Source: https://internetworldstats.com/stats7htm © Miniwatts Marketing Group.

RELATIONSHIPS, BEHAVIOUR AND CLASSROOM CLIMATE

It is important to get the classroom climate right for the learning of languages. This includes the classroom decor, set-up and arrangement, as well as the emotional, social and physical aspects of the space. Teachers influence learners' behaviours and attitudes to learning, so a negative classroom climate can feel hostile, chaotic or out of control. A positive classroom climate feels safe, respectful, welcoming, inclusive and supportive of learning.

I remember during my first interview for a job as an MFL teacher, when I had not yet graduated, stating clearly that when students stepped into my classroom I wanted them to feel like they had been teleported to a strange, interesting and distant land. You can organise your MFL classroom however works best for you. Having experimented with an array of set-ups and layouts, I worked out that what worked best for my classes was asking students for their opinions and noting subtle (and sometimes obvious) changes in behaviour. Allowing students to share their opinions about which arrangement they find most conducive can help to develop a positive classroom climate. This is particularly important for the MFL classroom, because students up and down the country have got the idea, perhaps from school leaders or parents, that MFL is:

- Too hard for them.

- Not an option for them because they aren't in the right option pathway.

- Not as important as [other subjects].

- Invalid and useless in the digital age.

- Pointless because everyone speaks English.

- Not required because technology will make MFL teachers obsolete (voice recognition, translation devices, automation, robots, etc.).

- Not required as they'll never visit [country].

- Not a good choice because it's easier to get a higher grade in [another subject].

And the list goes on.

I have chosen to ignore those comments, and continue greeting students with a smile and a *Bonjour*, *Guten Tag*, *Привет* or *Hola*. Their time in the MFL classroom is precious, and I want them to feel welcomed, happy, confident, enthusiastic and brave. I also want them to enjoy the experience of learning a language, whatever job or career path they choose. And students can most definitely make sounds, identify words, create sentences and paragraphs, have fun with grammar and make progress, and enjoy it, regardless of their ability. I believe that *all* learners can achieve in MFL, if given the opportunity and the right classroom climate.

The learning climate is paramount to building a professional teacher–student relationship, as well as easing fears and nerves if there is any anxiety. Key to this is creating the best possible educational environment and learning space – perhaps using the collection of items you have garnered from your reading and personal travels. There are some elements of the classroom that can't be changed, of course – fixtures, fittings, the size and position of windows and doors – but there is much that can. Creating interest using colourful, attention-grabbing displays and images is not particularly challenging but it does take time. However, this time is well-invested if the walls, doors, desks, shelves and ceiling all communicate your passion for and interest in the subject. I aspire to have my students hooked into the learning, captivated by the subject and eager to get on with what they are going to learn as soon as they enter the classroom.

The teacher also needs to be calm, confident, well-prepared, organised, focused, happy to see everyone and wearing a smile, which shows in the eyes and in positive body language. We need to acknowledge every student as they enter and head to their workspaces, discreetly scanning to check that everyone is present, correctly dressed and in the right mindset to learn and make progress. Your readiness and welcome will settle and guide your students in gauging the climate of the room. Distractions from outside the classroom need to be identified, addressed and, if possible, ignored: we don't want external concerns to materialise in the classroom and become a barrier to learning.

Giving students a task to get on with ensures that positive routines are established from the outset, and there is no loss of learning time while you complete the necessary paperwork. Clear routines ease anxiety and allow learners to 'warm up' to the MFL classroom. This is not sedately undisturbed waiting. This is an awakening of the senses and a warming up of their ears and eyes to languages. It is about helping the learners to get themselves MFL ready and to engage their languages brain. This is important because almost every other subject on the curriculum will be in their native tongue. The settling task should be a *pre*-starter to the starter which will launch the learning journey. We need to engage and awaken previous learning experiences – the vocabulary, syntax and grammar as well as the skills. Not even elite athletes like Usain Bolt, Owen Farrell and Nicola Adams could simply turn up and perform at a world-class level; they too need to warm up their bodies and minds and get themselves in the zone.

The pre-starter could be a Thunk,[7] a tantalising thought piece reflecting on cultural knowledge or a relevant news item from the day. It could be a translation to tickle their learning taste buds and chew over with their partner or alone. It could involve recalling vocabulary items, chunks or phrases from prior learning, a tense or important construction, or simply remembering what was learned in the previous lesson. The purpose is to encourage links to be made between previous learning and the learning to come, transporting students back, awakening their foreign language brain and forcing them to fire up frontal cortex neurons to electrify synapses.

Resources should be out and tasks ready. Should any learner not have their equipment, adopt a no-fuss approach of having spares available – rulers, pens, pencils, paper, whatever they need to get on with settling and learning. We don't always know about students' circumstances at home or outside of school, so we shouldn't humiliate or punish individuals for not having a pen or book. Classrooms should be safe spaces. If we shame students who don't have the right equipment, then the safe space disappears, and the learning climate isn't one of calm. Of course, there isn't an endless supply of resources, but there are simple ways to get hold of writing materials that don't require teachers to spend their own money. TeachMeets, conferences, exam boards, banks, insurance companies and shops all have freebie stationery; you just have to be brave enough to ask. I've done it for years! After all, no doctor, nurse, dentist or surgeon can complete their job without the right kit.

---

7   A Thunk is a beguilingly simple question which stops you in your tracks and encourages you to look at the world in a new light. For some examples see: I. Gilbert, *The Little Book of Thunks: 260 Questions to Make Your Brain Go Ouch!* (Carmarthen: Independent Thinking Press, 2007).

A positive teacher–student relationship starts with acknowledgement, care, trust and a smile. I find that great professional relationships are key to encouraging students to achieve more, both academically and linguistically. If we build strong relationships based on mutual respect, humanity, kindness, care and honesty, then compliance, positive engagement, risk-taking and progress will come. I learned this as a young MFL teacher with some delightful (and challenging) young people. If you fail to get the professional relationship right as a teacher, it can make for a tricky time.

In the last five years I've had some difficult classes which have tested my teaching skills and strategies, while also trying my patience and leading me to question my ability. Thankfully, I found the answer to my problems at the very first workshop I attended at the Northern Rocks Education Conference in 2014, led by a passionate and inspirational head teacher and behaviour specialist, David Whitaker, from Springwell Special Academy. David described the reasons or potential messages behind challenging behaviour and the concept of unconditional positive regard, and it immediately struck a deep chord.[8]

Springwell seeks to accept and value every learner, caring for them and responding to their additional learning and behavioural needs, but also helping them to remain in an

---

8   The concept of unconditional positive regard was developed by psychologist Carl Rogers. It involves the basic acceptance and support of an individual, regardless of what the person says or the behaviour they display within the context of therapy. The principles of unconditional positive regard are increasingly being applied in the education sector. It is helping teachers, TAs and FLAs to build positive relationships with learners by isolating unwanted behaviours from the individual who displays them, while still accepting, nurturing and caring for them and responding to their needs appropriately. See J. Benson, The Power of Positive Regard, *Educational Leadership* 73 (2016): 22-26. Available at: http://www.ascd.org/publications/educational-leadership/jun16/vol73/num09/The-Power-of-Positive-Regard.aspx.

educational setting. This is not easy: the structure, values and approaches in place at the school are robust, but they also seek to respond to the learners' behaviour, develop their confidence and expand their experiences, so better choices can be made. Kindness and unconditional positive regard go hand in hand, which changes learners' experience and makes a huge difference to every individual who attends this very special school.[9]

Passionately language focused, I'd lost sight of what was important, so from that point onward I promised myself that I'd refocus on repairing and building relationships with those students who needed additional attention, those for whom MFL was perhaps not their top priority. It certainly wasn't an overnight success, but because of my own philosophy, passion and zest for teaching and learning, and for young people and international languages, I just needed to make a few adjustments. Trust could be relearned and re-established. I was steadfast in this until the desired aim was achieved, which required all my skills and patience, and bucketfuls of care, kindness and unconditional positive regard.

It took somewhere between six and nine months, and I haven't looked back since. Reticent students started to respect their language learning and make excellent progress. Languages didn't magically transform to become the students' favourite subjects, but they had realised that they could learn in the languages classroom – it was achievable, it wasn't something else to fail. Over time they saw the value in the subject, and could – with effort and endeavour – find focus and develop their language knowledge, skills and understanding. The disruptive and challenging behaviour subsided, and a positive classroom

9   J. Halliday, 'We Batter Them with Kindness': Schools That Reject Super-Strict Values, *The Guardian* (27 February 2018). Available at: https://www.theguardian.com/education/2018/feb/27/schools-discipline-unconditional-positive-regard.

based on mutual respect, kindness, hard work and learning was restored.

STUDENT VOICE AND ENGAGING THE DISENGAGED

Engaging disengaged students can be challenging but it pays dividends to do so. As much as I love teaching languages, not all students leap out of bed and dash to school with a bounce in their step, ready to learn because of languages. There are numerous reasons why this is, but one tool I have always used to help me is harnessing the power of student voice. Asking students their opinion can provide wonderful insight into the happenings in your classroom and in your students' minds. It also helps to reinforce learners' feelings of worth, belonging and trust, boosting their self-esteem and making them feel acknowledged and valued for their contributions to developing the languages experience and curriculum. Student voice has helped me to make changes and adjustments to my classroom pedagogy, my practice and the language learning curriculum for the better.

A student questionnaire doesn't need to be onerous – just a few key questions can yield valuable information that can be used to improve and develop the learning environment for the better. There is also the one-to-one conversation to find out exactly why individual engagement isn't as it should be. After all, students experience multiple subjects across a school day – across a school week they can have 25 or more lessons. Their contact with different teachers across various subjects can provide a wealth of information which we can tap into the MFL classroom. Co-constructing a curriculum with students

Language: _____

Teacher: _____

Year group: _____

Please answer the following questions below.

1 = Never, 2 = Rarely, 3 = Sometimes, 4 = Frequently, 5 = Always

1.	My teacher shares where the class is going, what we are learning and why.	1 2 3 4 5
2.	My teacher explains content and materials clearly.	1 2 3 4 5
3.	My teacher indicates important points to remember.	1 2 3 4 5
4.	My teacher shows genuine interest in me and others in the class.	1 2 3 4 5
5.	My teacher effectively stimulates discussion and listens to me.	1 2 3 4 5
6.	My teacher provides helpful comments on my work and assessments.	1 2 3 4 5
7.	My teacher is tolerant of different opinions expressed in class.	1 2 3 4 5
8.	I can work effectively in the class.	1 2 3 4 5

9.	My teacher explains new concepts well so that I can understand.	1 2 3 4 5
10.	I am encouraged to ask questions and give answers in lessons.	1 2 3 4 5
11.	My teacher adjusts the pace of the lesson to my level of understanding.	1 2 3 4 5
12.	My teacher is well-prepared.	1 2 3 4 5
13.	My teacher gives additional help, support or challenge when I need it.	1 2 3 4 5
14.	My teacher treats me and others in the class with respect.	1 2 3 4 5
15.	My teacher helps me to learn.	1 2 3 4 5
16.	My teacher meets and greets me in every lesson.	1 2 3 4 5
17.	My teacher uses a variety of resources in our lessons.	1 2 3 4 5
18.	My teacher smiles at me.	1 2 3 4 5
19.	I enjoy this subject.	1 2 3 4 5
20.	I am happy with the progress I am making in this subject.	1 2 3 4 5

can be a truly wonderful experience. On pages 24–25 there is an example of one of the many questionnaires I have used with my students.

More recently (thanks to some fabulously creative people who have shared templates on Twitter and Instagram) I have used questionnaires to ask students to give feedback on a series of lessons or projects. Students love the opportunity to feed into the learning experiences of others, particularly their younger peers. I truly believe that co-construction is a force for good, providing you prepare your class in advance (it really does require trust), really listen and act on the information given to you. If the learners in your classroom trust that you will not belittle or ignore their suggestions, then they will give feedback freely and honestly. This will enable you to engage your learners better, improve the learning experience for others and give you an insight into the brilliant things that colleagues in other departments are doing.

I'm aware that some teachers and teaching unions disapprove of student questionnaires, but I use the information gained purely for reflective practice. I'm not a people-pleaser or a teacher-entertainer, but I do want my students to enjoy their language lessons, develop a love for the subject, be curious about the new words and phrases they encounter, and become better and more confident linguists. Bear in mind that you might not like everything you hear, but it brings problems out into the open and gives you an opportunity to discuss them and build relationships. The questionnaires can be anonymous if you prefer, but I have found that students are often happy to include their names.

Exit tickets (like the example on page 27) are another fabulous resource, providing instantaneous feedback about what students would like to learn more about or what they would like more practice at or what additional support they would like. Simple yet brilliant. I've used exit tickets with Key Stage 4 and 5 students at the end of the lesson to ensure that I know what they need. It's part of the plenary and provides a progress journey for the learners themselves to reflect on and develop independently. It is especially valuable when learners are given enough time to provide an extended answer after a project or series of lessons in the target language. If you haven't already tried it, please do – you might be surprised by what your students come back with.

Date:	Name:
What I have learned today:	
What I'd like more practice at (and what support I'll need):	

Both questionnaires and exit tickets are excellent techniques, but think carefully about what you want to learn from your students. Some teachers have moved on from student questionnaires to learning diaries, two-way dialogue in the back of exercise books or whole-class conversations. The important thing is that we speak to our learners to ensure that the plans, activities and projects we create meet their learning needs.

Unless we film ourselves as practitioners, we don't always see ourselves teaching. We might have a perception of how we believe we are as languages teachers in the classroom (perhaps based on how we've seen teachers portrayed in films), but teaching isn't like that in reality. It has certainly taken more than 90 minutes to get a tough new class to trust me and to do the work set, although I am firmly of the belief that 'everything that you put in, the children always return it,'[10] so take the time to get to know the young people in your classes, build positive professional relationships with them and involve them in their MFL learning journeys. Ultimately, you know what is best for your learners, but the power of student voice can have a tremendous impact on your practice and, of course, on your relationships in a professional capacity.

Ensuring that you treat each student with dignity and respect and extend unconditional positive regard when facing disengagement or challenging behaviour is a sure-fire way to build positive relationships and help engage disaffected learners. However, these are powerful long-term approaches, so some quicker strategies you could employ include:

1 Plan B. Make sure you have alternative back-up activities for struggling, anxious or upset learners, so they are still learning and involved in the lesson.

2 Spare seat/safe space. If you have detected that a learner isn't in the mood or is upset, set aside a quiet space where they can go – so their distress isn't in full view of others – and complete their work in peace. This

---

10 Georges Lopez in *Être et Avoir*, dir. N. Philibert (2002).

allows students to have a calm place to be while remaining in your classroom.

3   Back-pocket task. It is a fact that students don't always complete every single task. I make my expectations clear in September and January – a small reminder to us all of what we do around here. I then ask the students to construct a 'back pocket' in their exercise books for loose items, quizzes, worksheets, speaking mats,[11] extension/enrichment tasks and any unfinished items. The students can go through their back-pocket tasks at those times when they feel unable to engage with the main activity. This enables the learner to stay on track and continue engaging with languages.

4   Lolly stick task. If you use lolly sticks in your classroom for extension or enrichment tasks for early finishers, you could ask the student to select a stick and complete the designated activity.

5   Reading. Language magazines are always useful if a student needs quiet time. Allow them to select one and read it for a little while. This enables them to continue to access the language and gives them time to reconnect with the lesson. If I employ this strategy, I expect the student to complete a 3-2-1 activity: noting down or telling me three things about the articles they have read, two new words/phrases they have picked up and one amazing fact or idea they have discovered while reading.

6   A–Z task. Ask the student to identify at least 26 vocabulary items, one for each letter of the alphabet. It could be either a single item of vocabulary on a specific topic or as many items of vocabulary as they

---

11 Speaking mats include useful words, phrases, expressions and key linguistic structures to help learners improve their confidence in speaking and develop their range, variety and depth of language.

can come up with for each letter (with the stipulation that they must have at least one word for every letter first).

I have found these six activities to be incredibly useful. They all seek to engage the learners in language while also respecting the fact that they may not be able to participate in the primary lesson activity; equally, they don't allow the student to disengage or disconnect from languages completely. This is important. Sanctioning quiet time in this way respects the learner and their psychological or emotional state. It also reinforces the teacher–student relationship, ultimately building trust and resilience. Relationships matter.

CHAPTER 3
LANGUAGE SKILLS AND ORACY

Encouraging students to speak in a second language can become increasingly difficult as they advance through secondary school, so it is useful to develop a toolkit of strategies to help keep spoken language activities interesting, engaging and relevant. The range of strategies is important: we don't want students to become bored with the same exercise. Language learning experiences need to remain fresh, exciting and rewarding. Keep them wanting more, I say!

The expectation that students will be able to speak in a second language as a result of simply repeating exercises fails to recognise that there are several aspects to developing speaking skills which are generally not taught. These include using the speech patterns, sounds and rhythms of another language to form words and phrases, and pronouncing these correctly. The ability to speak in another language is a life skill: the aim is to be able to convey information and instructions as well as personal thoughts and opinions. Communication through sound is the first form of communication every human makes, and this develops into speech patterns over time. We should not assume that learners can do this in a second language with confidence and proficiency without modelling and explaining to them what we expect and without creating an environment where the stepping stones to successful oracy are clear, attainable and worthwhile.

As MFL practitioners, we must ensure that learners know a language well enough to be able to think of an appropriate phrase or construct a logical sentence or longer piece of text. In order to do this, they need to have a sound understanding of grammar and a good range of vocabulary. They must be able to communicate their message with confidence and fluency through spoken and written forms. They also need to be able to listen to an oral piece and read a text, which requires decoding and translating strategies between two languages, as well as a good application of logistical reasoning. All of this is built up through careful and successful learning experiences which inform progress through ongoing formative assessment, culminating in the successful completion of end-of-unit tests and formal examinations. This requires a thorough modelling of the language. We don't want to overwhelm students, but they do need to be sufficiently immersed in the language such that they are familiar with it and can identify it and break it down, both when listening and when reading.

DECODING

When teaching an international language, we have to coach students to decode the words they see and the sound patterns, rhythms and intonation they hear. If they don't, they will decode the word using their native speech sounds and patterns, which results in anglicised language that is heavily influenced by their native tongue. Teaching phonics and then grapheme–phoneme relationships is vital if we are to avoid this problem. Students should be able to pronounce words correctly when asked to read aloud. This will have a huge impact when they are completing listening tasks and listening to their teacher speak in an international language. It will also impact on their confidence, as they will have a significantly improved chance of accessing the language they hear and isolating and identifying words, chunks and phrases, which in turn will help them seek out answers.

There are many resources out there to aid language teaching in schools, but the most important point is that what is taught must be taught more than once and then recalled through practice activities in order to be learned and remembered, whether this is listening, speaking, reading or writing. Being able to read what you see and being able to make a link between what you hear and what you read is essential. This skill is not to be underestimated, so time must be allocated to teaching and recalling the grapheme–phoneme link in order that all learners can decode the language they see and hear.

PHONICS

Phonics programmes are designed to teach learners to listen to spoken language and identify phonemes – the smallest elements of a word which when put together form the correct pronunciation. In simple terms, this involves matching sounds with corresponding letters and groups of letters. International languages have different phonemes (there may be similarities but they are not transferable), so phonics programmes differ for each language. If learners are unable to link phonemes with written words, they will struggle to make connections to the language they see and hear. Instead, they will read the words in their native/first language. Programmes (such as Les Planètes Phoniques, Die Phonetikplaneten and Los

Planetas Fonéticos[1]) can be used effectively and enjoyably with learners across a range of classes. They are memorable, great fun and contain innovative and clever tongue-twisters and songs that aid and reinforce the learning of key sounds.

Nina Elliott (@senoraelliott) has created Hip Hop Phonics for her classes which I also highly recommend.[2] These active phonics workouts are superb and inspired.

Springwell Special Academy in the North of England has created Active Phonics, which is an award-winning programme to help learners cement their knowledge and reinforce key sounds by shooting basketball hoops while recalling and speaking the phonemes in front of them.[3] Although Active Phonics is not used in an MFL setting at Springwell, it can certainly be used to engage young linguists to learn or reinforce key sounds.[4] From my research I understand that students love using Active Phonics because they are practising verbalising graphemes with their corresponding phoneme sounds actively outside of the classroom. According to the students they are 'not learning' – they are shooting hoops and enjoying themselves. This is incidental learning[5] at its best.

Another way in which phonics can be reinforced, also inspired by the Active Phonics programme at Springwell, is through hopscotch: graphemes are laid on top of the numbers and the learners shout out the sounds as they play. Repeat active practice is great fun and provides

---

1 See http://www.trainingforlearning.co.uk/planetes_phonique.htm.

2 See https://www.slideserve.com/beulah/hip-hop-phonics.

3 See https://activephonics.co.uk.

4 See https://springwelllearningcommunity.co.uk/about-us/active-phonics.

5 'Incidental learning is unintentional or unplanned learning that results from other activities': S. Kerka, Incidental Learning: Trends and Issues Alert No. 18 (2000), p. 1. Available at: https://files.eric.ed.gov/fulltext/ED446234.pdf.

memorable learning experiences which the students find easy to recall and remember.

Repetition and drill exercises[6] are commonly used to introduce new language to learners in the MFL classroom. However, if they are not able to decode a word (by using the grapheme–phoneme link) this can impair language confidence and is likely to result in students being unable to securely identify words in the international language with their own/first language or with previously learned language. This is a missed opportunity. Confidence in listening, reading and speaking skills is boosted when phonemes are taught explicitly. Learners want to sound distinctive, so having good pronunciation when they speak a second language can extend and enrich their experience. By teaching them phonics, the students are able to access new and unfamiliar language in texts and are increasingly able to manipulate the language with growing confidence and success.

SPEAK IT, WRITE IT

I believe that if students can speak it, they can write it, especially with the strong foundation of phonics. Languages teachers do this partially in repetition and drill exercises when introducing new language. We should not shy away from insisting on correct pronunciation when students are speaking or reading texts aloud. However, it is important not to overcorrect and risk lowering learners' self-confidence – it is a delicate balance.

---

6   Drill exercises are used by teachers to introduce new language to students. The teacher says (models) the word or phrase and the students repeat it. Other types of drill include substitution drills or question and answer drills.

Students are more eager to respond to questions in the target language if they are confident that they sound like a 'native'. A reading aloud activity/game called 'Rhubarbe!' (see pages 43–44) supports and reflects this aspiration: their enthusiasm and motivation to engage are heightened as the fear of 'saying it wrong' is reduced. Students aren't afraid to try because they have been taught how to do so correctly. Question and answer sessions, role plays, picture-based oral tasks, presentations, classroom language and recital all become so much easier, more accessible and less fraught when learners are self-assured about their pronunciation.

PHYSICALITY AND PERFORMANCE

Phonics isn't the only speaking skill we have to address in the pursuit of encouraging confident oracy. Physicality and performance also need to be supported. Singers are taught how to breathe, how to create sound, how to use their voice box, mouth and lungs, and how to project safely; languages teachers should be doing this too. We need to teach students how to project their voice, how to stand or sit when speaking aloud, how to open their chests, how to relax their shoulders and how to speak calmly.

Some of my students have been anxious, especially in assessments, and end up speaking into their chest, hiding behind their fringe or struggling to sit still. This doesn't make for a great spoken piece that shows off their language skills. Spending time coaching students about posture – to have their heads up, shoulders back, mouths unobscured and making eye contact with the person they are speaking to – is extremely important. I have five simple rules:

1   Look at your audience (or past them).

2   No obstructions (such as hands, hair, pens, rulers, etc.) across your face.

3   No looking down.

4   Think pace, clarity and pronunciation.

5   Stand tall.

THE FOUR STRANDS OF ORACY

Loic Menzies, Will Millard, Amy Gaunt and James Mannion of School 21[7] and Cambridge University have done extensive research into the impact of oracy. Their work has led to a curriculum that is built around oracy and has had a dramatic impact on every learner at School 21. They have identified four strands (shown on page 38) which are crucial to developing good oracy and speaking skills with learners of all abilities.

The Voice 21 programme is a campaign to raise the status of oracy in schools across the UK and to get young people, with support from their teachers, talking in class.[8] The oracy framework, alongside the professional development training programme offered by Voice 21, provides support for teachers and their students to develop oracy in four key areas: physical, linguistic, cognitive, and social and emotional. When accentuated, monitored and tracked, these

---

7   School 21 is a state-funded and fully inclusive 4-18 school in Stratford, London which opened in 2012. It pioneers new pedagogies, especially in oracy. See www.school21.org.uk.

8   See www.voice21.org.

Use the oracy framework to understand the physical, linguistic, cognitive, and social and emotional skills that enable successful discussion, inspiring speech and effective communication.

Physical

Voice
- Pace of speaking
- Tonal variation
- Clarity of pronunciation
- Voice projection

Body language
- Gesture & posture
- Facial expression & eye contact

Linguistic

Vocabulary
- Appropriate vocabulary choice

Language
- Register
- Grammar

Rhetorical techniques
- Rhetorical techniques such as metaphor, humour, irony & mimicry

Cognitive

Content
- Choice of content to convey meaning & intention
- Building on the views of others

Structure
- Structure & organisation of talk

Clarifying & summarising
- Seeking information & clarification through questions/ing
- Summarising

Self-regulation
- Maintaining focus on task
- Time management

Reasoning
- Giving reasons to support views
- Critically examining ideas & views expressed

Social & Emotional

Working with others
- Guiding or managing interactions
- Turn-taking

Listening & responding
- Listening actively & responding appropriately

Confidence in speaking
- Self-assurance
- Liveliness & flair

Audience awareness
- Taking account of level of understanding of the audience

voice 21

THE ORACY FRAMEWORK

Source: School 21, used with kind permission.

skills can enhance the confidence, quality and level of students' spoken language.

In many traditional MFL lessons only two areas tend to be focused on when developing speaking skills: the linguistic and cognitive strands. Some consideration may have been given to social and emotional aspects, notably listening and responding, as well as confidence in speaking. But School 21 has highlighted additional areas within the social and emotional strand (working with others and audience awareness) and the physical strand. Once pointed out these four strands are obvious. I now use this diagram to ensure that I give learners the best possible opportunity to become confident language speakers.

The impact of focusing on the physical and social and emotional strands has been dramatic, particularly on students' use of voice, body language and posture. There have also been striking changes to student confidence and clarity across the age and ability ranges. These changes did not take long to effect – after modelling expectations with my students the transformation has been swift and impressive.

A vital element of my classroom practice has always been to encourage and remind students to listen actively in a group situation, and to obtain proof of this by giving feedback to the speaker or by completing a 3-2-1 activity. Not only does this improve the performance of the speaker, but it also develops the listening skills of the designated partner or other members of the group. It also promotes the social conventions of turn-taking and not interrupting the speaker. These are small but distinct shifts that have had a dramatic impact on the development of language skills in my classroom.

GROUND RULES

When using the four strands of oracy to promote high-quality speech and debate, I always set some ground rules and take the time to explain these to the students. I want active yet focused speakers, and focused yet active listeners. Students learn marvellously from one another by stealing fantastic phrases, complex constructions and valuable vocabulary, which they can then use to develop their own spoken pieces.

My ground rules for speaking are:

- Articulate clearly and project your voice – speak to the back of the room.

- Stand tall with shoulders back and chest open.

- Make eye contact – don't look down.

- Remember to breathe.

- Pace yourself – don't rush.

- Use punctuation as a pause.

- Stay calm.

- Try not to fidget.

- Empower others to join in.

And for good listeners:

- Prove you are listening.

- Respect the speaker – listen carefully and don't interrupt.

- Be prepared to ABCi (add, build, challenge or interrogate) another speaker about something you have heard.

- Respond to the speaker by politely answering any questions asked or comments made.

- Collect information or language (vocabulary or grammar) you find interesting using a 3-2-1 activity.

- Collate feedback on others' spoken pieces, giving comments which are kind, specific and helpful to improve future performances.[9]

Ensure that there are plenty of opportunities for students to practise speaking skills throughout the scheme of learning.[10] You should also aim to use a range of activity types to encourage and support reticent speakers. If students become confident speakers and orators, they will value using their voice to express opinions, give instructions, share creative pieces and make comparisons between personal and factual experiences. Sharing detail about their passions, lifestyle and culture is empowering, but it also develops and improves engagement, cognition, recall, fluency, linguistic range and depth.

DEVICES TO AID SPEAKING IN THE MFL CLASSROOM

Time is precious in the MFL classroom, and curriculum constraints don't always allow enough time for students to hone an amazing performance. Time-saving measures

---

9   See R. Berger, *Critique and Feedback: The Story of Austin's Butterfly* (8 December 2012) [video]. Available at: https://www.youtube.com/watch?v=hqh1MRWZjms.

10 A scheme of learning is a plan of learning across a year or key stage comprising the structure, content and language of a course. It maps out the intended learning and gives clear support and guidance for teachers. This is not an interpretation of an exam syllabus; it is an expectation of what learners will learn throughout the course.

include the use of digital devices: speaking tasks or performances can be recorded if students are fortunate enough to have their own device (mobile phone, Apple watch, tablet, GoPro, MP3 player, etc.). Increasingly, students have their own YouTube channels, so they can record speaking tasks or homework and upload it to their channel or Dropbox account. Self-publishing work on social media platforms dramatically increases the quality of student output. For those who do not have access to digital devices, try putting students in pairs and loaning them a school device to capture their pieces.

Apps enable students to edit, recreate, self-correct and improve their oral output, and many students appreciate the privacy they get from producing work in this way (you can use the privacy settings to share with teachers and not a wider audience). Some of my classroom favourites are YAKiT Kids, Apple Clips and, of course, YouTube (there are many more). In terms of safeguarding students online, ensure that they and their parents/carers are clear on the expectations of the task, as well as the implications of publishing their work online.[11] Reminding yourself of your school's safeguarding policy, with specific reference to online platforms, is vital to avoid anyone being placed in a vulnerable position. Support from home is crucial, so ensure that you communicate your expectations to students, parents and carers clearly and frequently. But you will need to provide alternative methods of completion, just in case.

---

11 Safeguarding is the process of 'protecting children from maltreatment, preventing impairment of children's health or development, ensuring that children grow up in circumstances consistent with the provision of safe and effective care, [and] taking action to enable all children to have the best outcomes.' Ofsted, *Working Together to Safeguard Children: A Guide to Inter-agency Working to Safeguard and Promote the Welfare of Children* (July 2018). Ref: DFE-00195-2018, p. 6. Available at: https://www.gov.uk/government/publications/working-together-to-safeguard-children--2.

FUN WITH SPEAKING AND ORACY

Developing oracy and offering opportunities to participate in speaking tasks in class are important, so here are eight fantastically engaging pair and small group tasks which are part of my repertoire.

1. RHUBARBE!

The aim of this superb oracy game is for the whole class to read through a text with perfect pronunciation, applying previously learned knowledge about the link between graphemes and phonemes.

Give the students a second language text – this could be a parallel text (with the English translation alongside it) to avoid too many questions about meaning. This will be a task that everyone participates in, so nominate a person to start and indicate who will go next. The first person reads the first sentence aloud, with the other students directed to follow (it helps to maintain focus if they use a ruler, pen or bookmark to follow the text). If a student reads their sentence correctly, they are congratulated, and then the second student reads the next sentence, and so on. If a student makes a pronunciation error, their peers are expected to pick up on this. When their classmate reaches the end of the sentence they should call out 'Rhubarbe!' The caller is expected to identify, explain and correct the pronunciation error. When this happens, the next student has to reread the previous sentence and avoid the error. This continues around the classroom until all the students have had the opportunity to read aloud and to practise listening and recall.

There are few students who don't love this game. It is highly engaging and encourages careful thought and focus – they always have to be on the alert. The students also enjoy taking the texts home to practise reading aloud. Practising the relationship between graphemes and phonemes in this way may recall phonics work from Year 7 – or indeed from beforehand, thanks to our primary colleagues. It enhances their access to a range of texts and, of course, promotes reading. The willingness of everyone in the class to succeed is palpable, so much so that, regardless of age, the students are often on the edge of their seats and any visitors can feel the enthusiasm in the room.

2. LONGEST SENTENCE/ BEST SENTENCE

This is an oracy or writing task in which students are given a topic, question or title. At the end of a period of thinking time they must construct the longest sentence they can. This can take a few minutes: not so long that they become distracted from the task but long enough that they have a response. You know your learners, so ensure they have the time they need for it to be a success.

If a speaking task: the students are encouraged to improve on their previous time, producing their sentence quicker but still ensuring that it makes sense They are allowed watches and access to digital devices to help them time the task.

If a writing task: the students are expected to write on alternate lines and create an interesting and engaging sentence. The language they use must be structured around the following mnemonics:

- CORTED: connectives, opinions, reasons, time-frames/time indicators and extra details.
- TAILORED: time-frames/time indicators, adjectives, intensifiers, linking words, opinions, reasons and extra details.

Languages teachers tend to use lots of mnemonics. In my department, we opted to use these to develop the students' spoken and written language but also as a guide to help them decode reading and listening tasks.

We provide tables for learners to stick into the centre pages of their exercise books for future reference. They are taught how to use the tables and are expected to employ a range of the phrases in speaking and writing tasks. The CORTED example on pages 46–47 is aimed at Year 7 learners, and the TAILORED table at students from Year 9 through to GCSE.

Following departmental discussions, these are key phrases that we wanted our learners to be able to read, know and use from early on. With expectations set high, the students worked hard to incorporate the language into their work. From Year 7, they were using some of these phrases and spelling and pronouncing them correctly. Furthermore, the students began to use the tables rather than asking for teacher support or a bilingual dictionary, thereby increasing independence and resilience across all classes and across the whole ability range. The students report that they like using the tables because they contain a range of everyday words and phrases as well as language that encourages diversification. Parents also value the tables as they support them in helping their children and boosting their independence.

CORTED

Connectives	Opinions	Reasons	Time-frames (present and future)	Extra details – adverbs	Extra details – high-frequency words and questions
Simple:	J'aime = I like	C'est bon/ intéressant/ facile/excellent/ génial/ fantastique = It's good/ interesting/ easy/excellent (/great)/ brilliant/ fantastic	tous les jours = every day	normalement = normally	j'ai = I have
et = and	Je n'aime pas = I don't like		une (deux) fois par jour = once (twice) a day	en général = generally	je suis grand(e) = I am tall
mais = but	Je déteste = I hate		le mois prochain = next month	souvent = frequently/ often	je suis fatigué(e) = I am tired
parce que = because	Je préfère = I prefer		la semaine prochaine = next week	généralement = generally	je suis triste = I am sad
aussi = also	J'adore = I love		l'année prochaine = next year	d'habitude = usually	je suis content(e) = I am happy
si = if	Je pense (que) = I think (that)			de temps en temps = from time to time	j'ai besoin de = I need to
également = also	Je crois (que) = I believe (that)				je dois = I have to/must
cependant = however	à mon avis = in my opinion				je veux = I want
					je préférerais = I would prefer

46

Complicated:	*pour moi* = for me	*C'est nul/ ennuyeux/ difficile/ barbant/ agaçant* = It's rubbish/boring/ difficult/boring/ annoying	*chaque matin* = every morning	*quelquefois* = sometimes	*je peux* = I can
bien que = although	*Je m'intéresse à* = I am interested in			*ne ...jamais* = never	*je voudrais* = I would like to
donc = therefore	*Je suis passionné/e de* = I am passionate about			*toujours* = always	*je vais* = I'm going to
peut-être = maybe/perhaps					*il y a* = There is/are
comme = such as					*ils/elles sont* = they are
où = where					*il/elle/c'est* = he/she/it is
quand = when					*Tu es ...?* = Are you ...?
que = which/that					*Tu as ...?* = Do you have ...?
					Il y a ...? = Is/are there ...?

TAILORED

Time-frames	Adjectives	Intensifiers	Linking words	Opinions	Reasons	Extra details
tous les jours = every day	*grand(e)* = big	*un peu* = a little	*et* = and	*je pense (que)* = I think (that)	*parce que* = because	**Time-frames – include time of day:**
une (deux) fois par jour = once a day (twice)	*petit(e)* = little	*assez* = quite	*mais* = but	*je crois (que)* = I believe (that)	*car* = because	*le matin* = morning
	gros(se) = fat	*très* = very	*parce que* = because		*c'est intéressant* = it's interesting	*l'après-midi* = afternoon
	mince = thin	*trop* = too	*aussi* = also	*à mon avis* = in my opinion		*le soir* = evening
le mois prochain = next month	*de taille moyenne* = average size	*extrême-ment* = extremely	*si* = if		*c'est facile* = it's easy	*Samedi matin à 9h ...*
la semaine prochaine = next week	*joli(e)* = pretty	*vraiment* = truly	*également* = equally	*pour moi* = for me	*c'est cool* = it's cool	*Dimanche après-midi à 15h ...*
l'année prochaine = next year		*vachement* = amazingly	*cependant* = however	*le/la meilleur(e)* = the best thing is	*c'est excellent* = it's excellent/ great	Descriptions of people (names, ages, number) – adjectives:
			malgré = in spite of	*c'est ...*		*Mon père, qui s'appelle George, est amusant.*
			bien que = although			*Mes deux frères, Jacques et Thomas ...*

le mois dernier = last month

l'année dernière = last year

la semaine dernière = last week

quelquefois = sometimes

de temps en temps = from time to time

rarement = rarely

fréquemment = frequently

---

laid(e) = ugly

jeune = young

vieux/vieille = old

fort(e) = strong

faible = weak

long(ue) = long

court(e) = short

propre = clean

sale = dirty

---

incroyablement = unbelievably

complètement/totalement = completely/totally

pas du tout = not at all

---

donc = therefore

peut-être = maybe/perhaps

tant que = while

comme = such as

où = where

quand = when

que = which/that

surtout = above all

même si = even if

y compris = including

---

le/la pire c'est = the worst thing is

ce que j'aime = what I like

ce que je n'aime pas = what I don't like

je m'intéresse à = I am interested in

ma passion est = my passion is

j'adore = I love

---

c'est passionnant = it's exciting

c'est moche = it's ugly

c'est ennuyeux = it's boring

c'est difficile = it's difficult

c'est barbant = it's boring

c'est nul = it's rubbish

Ma petite sœur, Amélie, a 7 ans.

Negatives:

ne ... pas = not

ne ...jamais = never

ne ... plus = no longer, not any more

ne ... rien = nothing, not anything

ne ... personne = nobody, not anybody

ne ... guère = hardly

ne ... aucun(e) = not any, none

ne ... que = only

ne ... ni ... ni ... = neither ... nor ...

ne ... pas encore = not yet

Time-frames	Adjectives	Intensifiers	Linking words	Opinions	Reasons	Extra details
	industri-el(lle) = industrial *moderne* = modern *ancien(ne)* = ancient *chic* = trendy	*J'adore le français car le prof est très sympa et je suis assez forte en ça. Je n'aime pas l'EPS parce que je ne suis pas du tout en forme et je suis vraiment nulle en sports.*		*j'aime* = I like *je n'aime pas* = I don't like *je déteste* = I hate *je préfère* = I prefer	N.B. A reason can be another opinion – e.g. *J'adore le français parce que j'aime parler.*	

Students know a range of details are expected and, where possible, more than one tense. In order to make their work stand out they also need to use a range of interesting vocabulary and techniques such as humour, irony and intrigue. I once taught a student through to A level and he made it his *raison d'être* to always include a lighthouse in his work. It began when I first set this challenge in Year 9 and continued through to Year 13. His creations were legendary throughout the school. I have no doubt that he maintained this wonderful affectation at university and hopefully now in his adult life. The lighthouse made his spoken and written pieces original, memorable and full of intrigue – of course, developed by his creativity and linguistic ability. Granted, not all students will rise to the challenge in this way, but many of his peers responded by making their work less formulaic and more interesting. His was a mixed-ability group, so opportunity and motivation were the significant factors, not linguistic ability.

3. TWO TRUTHS, ONE LIE

This is a Marmite strategy: you'll either love it or hate it. I love it, and my students do too! Encouraging students to lie brings with it audible gasps of horror from fellow teachers, yet students can't quite believe their luck and ask, 'Really, Miss?' Give the students some thinking time to come up with three statements – two that are true and one that is a lie. The art is in not going for the obvious. Students enjoy the linguistic challenge of outsmarting their peers and their teacher by devising brilliant statements and revealing something a little obscure about themselves.

This task is motivational through the elements of competition and creativity. It can be used to reinforce grammatical structures, negatives, word order, key language, complex structures and so on. It also provides opportunities for incidental learning. It is an awesome takeaway strategy and can be used as a starter, filler or at a carefully considered moment within a lesson. It's rewarding for the creator but also for the thinkers who are tasked with seeking out the deception. I have also used this technique at conferences and seen some stunned expressions on colleagues' faces as they scramble to identify the lie among the three statements. Fabulous!

I understand that not everyone wants to encourage their students to lie, but this strategy is an inventive approach to motivate the development of stimulating classroom language and discussion. I explain to students that the lies have to be in the target language and remain in the classroom. They are absolutely clear that this isn't a carte blanche for dishonesty and should only ever feature in my classroom in the completion of this task.

4. ALL TALKING, NO WRITING

Depending on their level of experience, some students prefer to write responses to questions rather than speak them, despite the need to develop good oracy in MFL. On those occasions when a task requires all talking and no writing, the students need careful guidance and support when working in groups. It is a challenge for students to spend an entire lesson (or even a specified amount of time in a lesson) only communicating in the international language with their peers and teacher, but it is necessary if they are to develop spontaneity and oracy as well as purposeful peer-to-peer communication. The task could be a reading comprehension; producing a report, presentation, role play or question and answer session; locating the answers in a listening task or from watching a short video; or peer assessment – it's up to you to decide. But be clear:

no writing is allowed in the completion of the task, only speaking.

Initially, allocate short bursts of time to build up their confidence and ensure that sufficient thinking time is allowed. Discussion during the thinking time can be in the first or second language, but I always insist that the main task is completed in the second language. As everyone is collaborating in groups, even reticent or nervous students tend to take part because no one other than their partner or group members will be listening.

Students can interrogate one another if language is unknown without fear of holding up the class, with the bonus that the only audience is their group. Clearly grouping is important here, as is the timing of the task. Scaffolding through speaking mats or support on an interactive whiteboard may be required, but I find having something in front of them encourages the students to have a go rather than remain silent and stare longingly at their closed exercise book.

This strategy also allows more confident linguists to speak meaningfully to one another, so it is a stepping stone to the coveted student-to-student target language speaking.

5. TABOO

Taboo is a guessing game where the goal is for a player to get their teammates to guess the word they are describing without using the word itself or five other related words. It is great for developing linguistic skills and creativity in the international language. It is fun to use a random student selector, such as those collected together on www.classtools.net. Alternatively, the students can choose a lolly stick containing a taboo word or phrase which they have to describe to their peers.

As well as being exciting and highly competitive, taboo is perfect for practising key language and a reminder of what to do if you don't know the exact word to get your point across. It reminds me of a strategy my own MFL teacher taught me in preparation for my GCSE oral exam many years ago. I employed it when I couldn't remember the word for mirror: describing the object in the role play task allowed me to continue and gain some marks, despite not being able to remember the specific vocabulary.

It is also a useful strategy to employ when students are overusing a word or phrase. It can be used with all classes and levels and is a clever way to force students to use negative phrases and comparatives. Intense, hilarious fun – and all conducted in the target language!

6. PICTIONARY

Pictionary is like Taboo, except there is no talking from the artist: one player draws a picture and other group members guess what is being drawn. All guesses must come from the deducers (the learners who are guessing the answer) and only in the international language. It is the perfect game for recalling and revising key vocabulary and creates much hilarity across the classroom. The lolly sticks created for taboo can be used for this game too.

7. UNE MINUTE, S'IL VOUS PLAÎT/ EINE MINUTE, BITTE/UN MINUTO, POR FAVOR

Based on the fabulous Radio 4 game show *Just a Minute*, this strategy helps rid MFL orators of long pauses, ums and ers. Students are allocated a topic, and some thinking time, and then have to speak about it in the second language for a minute. The mini lecture has to be clear, well-paced, well-pronounced and without long pauses or repetition. Single word notes can be jotted onto sticky notes to assist, but only as a guide or plan.

I have a great affection for this game because the students are very motivated to listen carefully in order to identify any repetition and to give feedback. They are also on the lookout for 'super steals' (clever phrases or vocabulary that the listener can steal to improve their own work) along the way. The game helps to develop confidence, fluency, pace, range, spontaneity, and depth and diversity of language, while also shining a spotlight on longer pauses and the need to fill gaps.

Students can work in small groups to build up to delivering their one-minute lecture to the class. Other group members can assist if the speaker is floundering by interjecting with an opinion, 'Je suis d'accord parce que ...'/'Ganz meine Meinung, weil ...'/'Estoy de acuerdo porque ....' This gives the student some breathing space and an opportunity to catch up or be re-inspired by the interjection. It also allows others in the group to speak up.

Of course, there is no reason why this activity can't be renamed 'Trente secondes', 'Dreißig Sekunden' or 'Treinta segundos' – it will be just as exciting, motivational and fun.

8. TALKING DICE/STORYTELLING DICE/VERB DICE

Fabulously illustrated story dice are increasingly available on the high street and online to help inspire your students to be inventive with their storytelling, thereby improving their confidence, spontaneity, range and depth of vocabulary. Organise the class into groups of three or four and allocate dice to each group. Add thinking time and a timer and they're off! When you first use the dice, share your expectations and instructions, perhaps by modelling using them yourself.

Story dice are definitely worth the investment, as they can be used for developing oracy as well as for writing tasks. The randomness of the dice delights the students, but it also allows them to be as creative as their minds and vocabulary will let them. I have heard the most wonderful stories, monologues and discussions. As the teacher, this activity enables you to stand back and observe the students at work, intervening to provide support and feedback only when necessary.

FUN WITH QUESTIONING

A vital element in students developing confidence with spoken work is to become familiar with question formats. They need to be able to recognise a range of question stems, partial questions and statements as questions. The following eight strategies are marvellous for encouraging students to be ready to ask or respond to questions asked in the target language.

1. POSE, PAUSE, POUNCE, BOUNCE

Question-and-answer sessions in the MFL classroom can be high frequency, yet as teachers and lead learners we shouldn't accept the first answer given. This encourages students to be ready for questions, to listen to their peers and to be ready to answer. Pose, pause, pounce, bounce is a widely used strategy (which was originally created and developed by Pam Fearnley[12] and promoted by Dylan Wiliam[13]) to avoid teacher–student ping-pong.

Wiliam suggests that a question is *posed*, after which the teacher *pauses* to give the students some thinking time (at least ten seconds). The teacher *pounces* on a student for an answer and then *bounces* this to another student, with the expectation that the second student will add to, build on or challenge the first response. Teachers are keen on this strategy, students less so, partly because the first answer is not accepted as the final answer. However, with repeat practice this effective questioning strategy can develop richness and depth in students' answers.

With more able and confident linguists, I add 'interrogate' to the answer to push students to use a range of language, and so start a debate from the original question. Students are given the opportunity to ask additional questions to seek out a clearer answer to the original question. This does elicit more detail and requires a higher level of language and also a deeper understanding of the content being quizzed through this activity. Pose, pause, pounce, bounce is a fine strategy to adopt in any MFL classroom and with linguists of any age.

2. HOT SEATING

Students will be used to hot seating from experiences in other lessons, not least drama and history, but it can be great fun in the MFL classroom too. Students in the hot seat take on the role of a character and are interviewed by the rest of the group. You can decorate a chair, use the teacher's

---

12 Thank you to Pam Fearnley of Pupils First UK (www.qhist.com) who can be contacted at: pamb566@btinternet.com.
13 See D. Wiliam, PPPB - Pose, Pause, Pounce, Bounce [video] (8 September 2016). Available at: https://www.youtube.com/watch?v=TMBsTw37eaE.

chair or bring in an unusual chair. This strategy can be used from Year 5 through to Year 13 with learners of all abilities, providing the necessary preparation work is completed beforehand. It can be useful to allow the student in the hot seat to prepare some notes, so although this is a speaking task it can also double up as a writing task.

3. WHAT'S THE QUESTION?

Providing students with an answer forces them to identify the question. They can use a range of formal and informal question structures which they have previously learned and practised. This strategy encourages a wider understanding of vocabulary and language as well as a deeper understanding of content. It is excellent way to model responses and help students to decode assessment and exam questions with increasing proficiency and confidence. It also helps learners to understand the range and breadth of language that can be used in response to a question, thereby providing them with exemplar answers which they can manipulate and build on.

Remember that you can use students' answers as examples. This not only celebrates the learners' work and enables a range of texts to be created and shared with the class, but it also creates opportunities for feedback on how the piece could be improved or developed.

4. BRAINBOX

BrainBox is a wonderful game that will be familiar to many teachers and students. With phrases given in the target language and English and question prompts covering a range of topics, this exciting memory game can be a source of much linguistic fun and frustration, all in one. A player picks a card and then studies it for a set period of time before being asked a question from the back (decided on by a roll of the dice). If the answer is correct the player keeps the card, if not it is returned to the box. The player with the most cards wins.

The cards contain lots of information, vocabulary and images related to various languages. They are a great conversational resource and encourage the students to speak about a range of engaging topics in the second language. This activity (which can last for 5 minute or 20 minutes) promotes recall, linguistic transference, vocabulary and grammar skills, practice in asking questions and giving good answers, confidence, spontaneity and oracy skills. It is available in French, German and Spanish. See www.brainbox.co.uk/brainbox-range.

5. NEUF QUESTIONS/NEUN FRAGEN/ NUEVE PREGUNTAS

In a grid of nine boxes, devise questions on a topic, theme or a range of tenses and display these on an interactive whiteboard. Direct the students (individually or in groups) to read these through carefully and think about different responses before preparing their answers. Nine questions can be a writing or speaking task.

If a speaking task: direct the students to give a 30-second or one-minute response. Depending on the group, prompts and notes can be made in advance, but these must not be simply read out. This task is designed to encourage the students to speak with increasing spontaneity and fluency, as well as transferring language knowledge and skills across different contexts. Teachers can record the presentations using a digital device and play these back to students to provide support for any feedback given.

If a writing task: ask the students to prepare a response of a set length, reminding them to include interesting details and key structures, using the mnemonics CORTED or TAILORED (see Chapter 3). They can answer more than one question in their response. At the end of the time allocated, the students should place their responses on the whiteboard next to the questions they have completed.

Whether speaking or writing, students tend to enjoy nine questions simply because there aren't too many questions, and although there is a range of questions they aren't too random. Most students who have given me feedback say that they can always answer at least one question initially, which warms up their brain to the topic, and they then find they can give responses to other questions too. Students also like pushing themselves to use a range of negative and complex language constructions.

Nine questions can be used following a reading of a literary text, to practise exam techniques or as part of a reading comprehension. It's a great activity to use in the MFL classroom or as a homework task; I have found it highly successful in the recall and practice of a range of questions, grammar and vocabulary.

6. 21 QUESTIONS/21 FRAGEN/21 PREGUNTAS

In the famous parlour game, 20 questions, a player (the answerer) chooses a subject but does not reveal it to the other players (the questioners). The questioners take turns asking a question which can be answered either yes or no. If a questioner guesses the right answer, they win the game; if 20 questions are asked without being guessed correctly, the answerer has won.

My variant, 21 questions, is perfect for the MFL classroom. Place students into groups and ask them to devise 21 questions to ascertain the answer. The answer could be a key piece of vocabulary, a grammatical item, a sentence, a message, a paragraph, the learning objectives for the lesson, the homework and so on – it's up to you as the teacher. The students get to practise a range of question styles and recall key vocabulary, but they are also engaged in collaborative and incidental learning by being exposed to a range of different structures and vocabulary. Allow thinking time and collaboration for the best learning experience and levels of engagement.

7. SAC PERDU (LES OBJETS TROUVÉS)/GEPÄCKVERLUST/LOS OBJETOS PERDIDOS

This is a great task for promoting curiosity and sparking the students' imaginations. A lost bag has been found but there is no trace of the owner. The students have to look through the items in the bag and ascertain who it belongs to, what the owner has been doing (or will be doing) as well as other details based on the interesting items in the bag. Collaborative discussion in groups and the creation of a spoken or written piece can expose some fantastic possibilities, brilliant language and lots of eager participation. The teacher can reveal the items one by one or the students can have a hands-on sensory experience. This activity has been so successful that students have asked to make up their own 'sac perdu' at home to bring in for us to use in the classroom.

8. SECURITY SERVICES

Identify some security service agents in the class or within groups, handing out an appropriate hat/dark sunglasses/ ID badge and allocating a subject of interest (i.e. a student). Select a topic using either lolly sticks or a random selector from the superb www.classtools.net. (Alternatively, the topic could be pre-selected.) Subjects of interest are expected to answer all questions on an identified topic, giving as much detail as they can in their answers. The agents should secretly record their observations on a mini whiteboard, identifying whether key details have been given using CORTED and TAILORED. At the end of the task, the agents should pass on their feedback. This is another way of encouraging students to practise using question phrases with peers. The roles can be rotated so they focus on a range of topics in both roles. The students tend to enjoy this activity and have lots of fun with it.

FIFTY IDEAS TO IMPROVE WRITTEN WORK

As an NQT/RQT many years ago, I attended a training session where the trainer stated that students should not be writing much, or indeed at all, during the first term of their language studies. I was horrified. However, by the end of the session I had been convinced. Students should be learning to speak the language and not just copying it from the board. The trainer was right (he is still training and sharing the same message nearly 20 years on).

Copying from the board is boring, if overused, so it makes sense to give students time and space to develop their oracy skills from the outset. In a real-life emergency writing is unlikely to be the first skill required. In this scenario we just have to speak, usually with a compelling reason to do so. We must ensure that language learners can speak clearly and with confidence (without reading written work aloud). The development of writing skills is important, of course, but this can come later on.

When developing writing skills learners tend to want to be perfect. I remember that I did; I didn't want my work to be anything other than neat and accurate. The reality is that students' written work is seldom perfect, so it can be helpful for the teacher to indicate that they are happy to see a developed or improved piece of work – imperfections and all.

There are lots of strategies for developing confidence with written work using mini whiteboards, the windows, desks and outside spaces. (Just make sure you check with the site team and pre-warn your cleaner, so you don't get into bother. There was once an incident at my school which can only be referred to as 'chalkgate' – I can't say anything more!)

1. SENTENCE STRUCTURE

As teachers, what are we expecting from our students? We should be teaching learners what a sentence looks like in the international language: its component parts and how this differs from their native language.

2. SENTENCE STARTER

We need to help students to help themselves by giving them sentence starters and encouraging them to build the rest of the sentence based on what they have learned from other language activities in the lesson/previous lessons.

3. SENTENCE BUILDERS

Building sentences is easy in our first language, but initially many learners struggle with the seemingly obvious in an international language. As teachers we should support them to build sentences by breaking them down so they can be built up again. Sentence builders have been a part of textbook life for departments and teachers who have been teaching for a while, but those who have not had access to them may not realise how brilliant they can be. Sentence builder tables allow for easy substitution and enable language skills to develop quickly, providing they are used consistently.

4. BUILD ME A SENTENCE

Ask learners to create one sentence on a topic, or use phrases or chunks that you have recently taught or expect them to know. If they produce a short and not particularly interesting sentence, direct them to include a minimum of 10, 12 or 15 words. You could allow the students to use sentence builder tables or mats to begin with, but make sure you withdraw these at some stage so they can learn to create sentences independently and practise this.

5. CORTED/TAILORED SHEETS

Direct learners to develop their sentence structures by ensuring that all the sentences they create contain a connective, opinion, reason, time-frame/time indicator and at least one extra detail (CORTED) or time-frame/time indicator, adjective, intensifier, linking word, opinion, reason and at least one extra detail (TAILORED). Once they can do this, get them to pluralise the nouns (and, in time, correct the grammar). You can extend this task by requiring learners to add further extra details to make their sentences more unique and interesting.

6. WHAT I'M LOOKING FOR (WILF)

Explain and model what you expect learners to produce when asking them to write. We don't want to 'dumb down' work, but learners aren't always great at transferability. Although they may use WILF in a range of other subjects, make sure you demonstrate what you expect in MFL and remind them of this frequently. You can start by creating a model, eliciting the answer from the students and then displaying this for them to develop further.

7. WHAT A GREAT ONE LOOKS LIKE (WAGOLL)

Show students what an amazing piece of written work looks like: break down the component parts and display this for them to access, especially when reviewing or drafting their own work. Learners aren't mind readers: if we don't show them what excellence looks like, how can they create it?

8. BEST WRITTEN SENTENCE

This is the writing version of the speaking strategy. Ask the learners to create their very best sentence. This is a wonderful task which encourages great thinking and reflection on the key elements to include, plus a review of grammatical knowledge and word order. Best sentences can be on anything and should include a wide range of language because they are the very best sentences the students can craft. This can be done individually or in pairs.

9. LONGEST WRITTEN SENTENCE

Encourage learners to construct the longest possible sentence they can, either individually or in pairs. Make sure to give them sufficient thinking and preparation time. Once they have crafted their sentence, they should write the different elements on coloured paper strips to create a paper chain. Chunks and complex constructions are to be advised and championed here. The winner can be rewarded for having the longest paper chain sentence containing many different components – they can stretch for quite a distance!

This is a highly engaging and motivating task which is loved by young and older learners. It also doubles up as a speaking task and creates display materials for your classroom. I drape the paper chains around my room and, when the need arises, remind learners of what they can do when they put their minds to a task and focus.

10. BEST PARAGRAPH

This follows on from the best sentence task. Students soon learn to develop interesting details and linguistic constructions that simply won't fit into one sentence, so they can progress from one long sentence into several sentences containing a variety of language.

11. BEST CREATIVE PIECE

Variety of language, a range of constructions and originality are all highly prized in the MFL classroom, so I encourage my learners to be creative when completing written pieces. When I set the task I remind them that their work does not have to be 'true', but it should be astounding in originality and blow me and their classmates away. Learners of all ages adore this task and find it exciting to be given free rein, but make sure you allow enough thinking time and remind them to plan their piece by writing on alternate lines so they have the space to add extra text.

12. CONCERTINA STORY TIME

I started using concertina story time a long time ago. It proved a great success then and it still has the same appeal now. I invite students to create a brilliant sentence – of course, allowing them thinking and writing time first. You could use a prompt such as an opening paragraph or take inspiration from the class. The idea is that the students write a superb sentence to add to a class story which they jointly create fold by fold. The catch is that they don't know what the story is about – they won't know what has been added before or after their own sentence.

Send around multiple sheets of paper, making sure the paper is folded carefully so the next recipient can't read what has gone before. Ensure everyone has participated and then collect them in. The stories can be unveiled using a visualiser or iPad and read out to the class, often with hilarious consequences. Not only is this a lot of fun, but it also celebrates creativity, which the learners love. It can result in head-scratching, possible confusion and some tumultuous twists and turns, but always some fabulous language.

13. COMIC STRIP CONVERSATIONS

Comic strips provide learners with the opportunity to create something enchanting which uses the international language but also shares their passion and ingenuity. These can be surprisingly complex so the students may require support. Over the years I have collected and kept many examples as they are a joy to read. The comic strips can provide a real snapshot into learners' lives and interests outside of school, thereby creating new opportunities to connect with them.

14. MINI-BOOK ADVENTURES

A fantastic alternative to comic strip conversations are mini-books, which first I learned about from a fabulous MFL maestro on Twitter. Check out Clare Seccombe's wonderful presentation from ALL Language World 2013 and her advice on how mini-books can be created in the classroom to draw out language and provide a creative outlet for learners through the medium of writing.[14]

I have used mini-books across an array of classes and abilities. All learners enjoy generating pieces of work in a book format, so if you have not tried this please do so. One project idea for Year 7 is to create a resource for incoming Year 6s to help them in their language learning. I now have a delightful collection of books crafted by Year 7s about life at secondary school, the lessons and teachers, the food in the canteen, the school uniform and a dictionary/glossary of classroom language and phrases, as well as vocabulary booklets for themes we have covered throughout the year.

15. KILLER CONSTRUCTIONS

Killer constructions, or 'wow' words, are one of my more recent discoveries. Students should have at their disposal a gamut of intriguing or unusual words, phrases and constructions which they collect and use in their written and spoken work – for example, 'après avoir' and 'après être' phrases. Using these constructions creates wonderful results which can really show off their linguistic range and high level of understanding.

16. BANNED – THINK AGAIN

I don't want my learners' written (or spoken) work to be repetitive and always use the same range of phrases, so I sometimes ban the use of certain words and phrases to encourage them to find an alternative. Some students love it, some don't, but they all engage well and produce

---

14 C. Seccombe, Make It with Mini-Books, *Changing Phase* (22 March 2013) [blog]. Available at: http://changing-phase.blogspot.com/2013/03/make-it-with-mini-books.html.

some interesting options. Thinking beyond the first idea that comes to mind helps to develop their repertoire and has a positive impact on their work.

17. GAP FILL/CLOZE TASKS

Developing students' understanding of word and phrase types can only be a positive in the languages classroom, so what better task than a gap fill or cloze task where they need to fill in the missing language items? These can help to get them thinking about the construction of the sentence in front of them and the need to know about the different types of words available. Gap fill tasks can be badly done if the primary driver is guesswork, whereas if the learners know what type of words might be missing (or are in the box, if there is one) it will be a phenomenal help in the successful completion of the task.

Trapdoor tasks are similarly brilliant. Create a text made up of a few sentences, some of which have various possible endings. The students must decide which ending is correct by reading the text aloud. These tasks can be easily differentiated to extend the repertoire of some students, while also providing much-needed support for others. Trapdoor tasks are challenging and fun, but students are also learning to manipulate language and extend and enrich their vocabulary and grammar.

18. SCAFFOLDING

Writing frames are a tried and tested method of providing things like key vocabulary, a set of simple or complex phrases, a selection of opinions, connectives and so on for the different stages of writing, such as the introduction, first paragraph and conclusion. Frames can also be modified to support different forms of writing, such as a report, interview, role play, or a 100- or 200-word task. If we model what we expect our learners to produce when setting up a writing task, this should support them to achieve a successful outcome.

Providing scaffolding to assist in the formulation of answers to a question is also extremely helpful. It can provoke deeper and more interesting responses, as well as encouraging (over time) a wider range of language usage.

19. SENTENCE BUILDER MATS

Sentence builder mats and tables can help to develop students' written work by providing examples of different word classes. Not only do the mats promote cognition and careful thinking, but they can also help anxious learners to overcome their fears and develop more independence. The level of support can be adjusted as learners' confidence and language ability increases.

20. POETRY

Written work doesn't have to be a 'traditional' written piece of X amount of words. We can also encourage our learners to express themselves by writing a piece of poetry or a rap. They love the opportunity to be creative, which can lead to some very engaging and personal work.

21. RANDOM WORD SURPRISE

Give the students a list of wonderful words – these could be favourite language words or recently learned items/ phrases – and challenge them to include these terms in their work. This task requires thoughtful reflection on the piece they have crafted; making substitutions and additions is a great skill to acquire, and practice can lead to deeper understanding and better structure.

22. CAN YOU ADD?

Give the students a phrase, but rather than asking them to provide one positive or negative opinion, instead ask them to develop the phrase. What can they add to make it more interesting to the reader? If you use a mnemonic (e.g. CORTED), encourage them to check that all aspects of this have been included.

23. KEYWORD CHALLENGE

Do you have a list of keywords or key phrases? If so, ask the learners to go back through their work and see how many they have included. This helps students to diversify their work by encouraging rereading and development.

24. LEVEL UP

Rather than always using the same vocabulary, direct students to level up by adding variation to their written work by utilising different connectives, reasons or opinion phrases. It's up to you as the teacher to decide what level of language you are expecting to see. Remember to model this and show the learners what a great one looks like – perhaps create one in class together prior to allowing learners to work independently.

25. RESTRUCTURE

Direct learners to reread their written pieces. If all their sentences start in a similar way, encourage them to rework any that start with 'Je', for example, to create more interest and variety in their sentence structures.

26. EXEMPLIFY

Encourage your students to back up opinions and reasons in their written work with examples. Justification and exemplification help learners to add a range of additional information to written work and develop the structure and depth of language used. It is also useful for learners to build up a bank of concrete examples (in both written and spoken work) that they can refer back to when necessary.

27. NEW WORD SPOTTER

Ask learners to revisit their work and add new vocabulary items or phrases. Recycling vocabulary and grammatical constructs not only helps with transferability, but it also helps to improve confidence with using them. Urging learners to recall vocabulary can be a fun way to ensure that they don't become reliant on a limited range of language.

28. TREASURE CHEST

A former colleague and brilliant teacher directed her students to use the central double page of their exercise books to create a treasure chest – a collection of fabulous words and phrases to use in written and spoken work. Her learners used these treasure chests when planning writing and speaking tasks as well as in dedicated improvement and reflection time (DIRT) activities to develop their international language skills and range.[15] It's great to see a unique and personal glossary of wonderful words and phrases collected by each learner.

29. KNOW, WANT, LEARN(ED) (KWL)

Direct your classes to show you what they know by planning their writing tasks carefully: they should indicate what they already know about the task/topic/question, what they want to learn more about and what they have learned.

30. TWO TRUTHS, ONE LIE

As we saw in the section on speaking and oracy, two truths, one lie is an exciting and highly engaging game which develops a variety of language skills and promotes peer-to-peer speaking and language analysis. Challenge the students to create three sentences in the target language, one of which is a lie and two of which are true (these can be about anything at all). Give the learners some thinking and writing time and then ask them to identify each other's lies. This can be done in small groups or pairs, or as a whole-class activity.

---

15 For more on DIRT, see J. Beere, *Independent Thinking on Teaching and Learning: Developing Independence and Resilience in All Teachers and Learners* (Carmarthen: Independent Thinking Press, 2020), pp. 96-98.

31. PAIRS CHECK

Organise the students into pairs (or allow them to choose their partner) and get them to swap written work. Armed only with a highlighter or coloured pen, they should underline or highlight any errors they see. After a specified time, books should be returned for their owners to address the highlighted sections. This helps students to revisit and reflect on completed tasks and aids with error correction. This strategy works well with older learners but can be used with a range of ages and abilities.

32. RALLYROBIN[16]

Allocate students into groups and then set the task: to write a response (such as a report or interview) incorporating the ideas and suggestions of all group members. Allot some time for thinking, group discussion and writing. The piece can be written collaboratively, but to really challenge the learners they should each write their own version.

33. ROVING REPORTER[17]

Assign one learner to be the reporter for the lesson – give them a clipboard, pen and an investigator/reporter hat. Their job is to roam around the classroom and collect beautiful sentences, vocabulary items, complex phrases and interesting discussion that they have overheard. At

---

16 RallyRobin is a Kagan strategy. For more information see: G. Clowes, The Essential 5: A Starting Point for Kagan Cooperative Learning, *Kagan Online Magazine* (San Clemente, CA: Kagan Publishing, 2011). Available at: https://www.kaganonline.com/free_articles/research_and_rationale/330/The-Essential-5-A-Starting-Point-for-Kagan-Cooperative-Learning.

17 S. Kagan and M. Kagan, *Kagan Cooperative Learning* (San Clemente, CA: Kagan Publishing, 2009), p. 139.

the end of the lesson they should share the wonderful things they have picked up from their peers. As this work is shared with the whole class, the learners learn from one another and can make a list of things to include in their written work next time.

34. FAVOURITE WORD DISPLAY

Encourage learners to share their favourite international language words and collate these on a display (translated into English if necessary). Urge the students to use the words in written work to spice up their responses. There could be a small reward for the most words used. (Warning: if the students go too far with this their writing and speaking tasks can become very random but utterly hilarious!)

35. TWO STAY, ONE STRAY/ TEAM STEAL[18]

Set groups of students a writing task. Once they have completed it one student from each group should wander around the other groups to see if they can steal anything they might have missed. It could be an amazing phrase, a complex construction or an element they have forgotten to add. The students love to pinch items and develop their own pieces, upping their game and their initial offering. Remember that not all students like to freely share their hard work, so make sure they don't cover up their prized pieces.

---

18 Kagan and Kagan, *Kagan Cooperative Learning*, p. 138.

36. BE NEGATIVE

Every so often, I like to remind my students of the scope of negative phrases by setting a head-scratching whole-class task to create a written piece using only negatives. The students' originality can be insanely imaginative and their tenacity unbelievable. It is also a great way of recalling, recycling and revisiting previously learned language.

37. CAUSE A FUSS

I sometimes set my learners the challenge of causing a fuss or argument with their controversial (or different) opinions. This task requires the students to craft an opposing response to a statement using complex and interesting vocabulary, even though it might be untrue.

38. CHANNEL YOUR INNER JACK

Encourage learners to identify and use an array of impressive linguistic statements, idiomatic phrases and anecdotes (think of my former student and his fascination with lighthouses) in their written work by emulating well-spoken and eloquent celebrities, comedians and inspirational heroes with whom they identify. This can lead to some fabulous pieces when the expressions are used correctly, delighting the reader and drawing them in with extra details. This also makes a great revision strategy (see Chapter 7).

39. WHAT'S YOUR END POINT?

When setting up a writing task, direct the learners to decide what the end point will be and plan it carefully. Ask them to consider what the reader will know on reading it that they didn't know before. This task encourages careful and logical planning as well as thorough checking to ensure that written pieces reflect what the learner set out to achieve. When they have finished the work, the learners should evaluate it against their plan to make sure they have not missed anything out. Practising these skills is vital if the students are going to produce good quality written pieces, especially under test conditions.

40. PLANT A FEW QUESTIONS

Support learners to produce clearly written work by encouraging them to ask themselves or their peers questions at certain stages of the writing process. In doing so, they are reflecting on the work they have already read and completed as well as demystifying their responses and/or developing the complexity of their work. Of course, they can also use the questions to assist with the completion of writing tasks, thus recycling key language and constructions to improve accuracy and competency.

41. DUAL CODED

Dual coding is based on the idea that forming mental images helps students to learn. Encourage your learners to reread and evaluate their written work and then draw small images in the margins, which will help to deepen the learning. (Students often end up adding images to their written work because they want to draw something ace for the reader!) This is a great task to promote reflection on written work beyond simple checking for accuracy.

42. INVERSION PLEASE

Rather than every sentence starting with a personal pronoun followed by a verb, advise your learners to switch this around by creating different and more interesting sentence structures. This is a simple yet challenging undertaking which is superb for developing the range and depth of language used.

43. 30/50/100 WORDS

Create short tasks for class work or homework which require the learners to create powerful and interesting written pieces of a specific length. The challenge here is to use precise language to communicate a specific message. This is excellent preparation for Key Stage 4, but it can also be used much lower down the school to develop an understanding of what 50 or 100 words look like. These tasks are great with younger learners to show them how much information can be included initially, and how precise they need to be to convey the key components in a clear and concise way. This is also a useful revision strategy (see Chapter 7).

44. SHOW ME WHAT YOU KNOW

Ask the students to complete a writing task, setting out the criteria clearly, explaining and modelling what a great one looks like (your expectations of their output), allowing planning time and sharing the success criteria. It all seems very obvious, but make it evident so the learners know exactly what they have to do to succeed. It's then up to them if they choose to take the hints and advice. If they don't do it this time, then I'm sure they will next time (with some feedback).

Show me what you know is a challenge but it's a warm and unthreatening one. Using this type of language, rather than a more formal writing assessment or test, helps learners to ease into the task and avoid those anxious feelings which can impede their success. This is another fantastic revision strategy (see Chapter 7).

45. KNOWLEDGE ORGANISERS

A knowledge organiser sets out important facts or information on a specific topic or unit, usually on a single page of A4 or A3. These can vary between subjects, but in MFL it might consist of a parallel text with a list of key vocabulary to identify and learn by rote, or a complex grammar or vocabulary list or even a speaking mat. However you use them with your learners, encourage them to regard knowledge organisers as a scaffold when structuring their written pieces, checking their work for accuracy or thinking of alternatives for overused language.

46. WRITE A LINE, MISS A LINE

As we've seen, it's a good idea to direct learners to write on alternate lines. This means there is space for them to add in extra elements later on should they need to, and it ensures that their written work is presented clearly. Learners warm to this method once they are used to it because it avoids scribbled additions and corrections.

47. GREEN PEN TIME

Some call it drafting; others call it green pen time. It doesn't matter what you call it providing the students are given time to check through their written work and add any additions or corrections in green. The whole piece doesn't have to be rewritten. It's great for teachers to see how the work has developed and been extended, and when. Give the learners your success criteria so they know what to check for and what should be included.

48. CH-CH-CHECK IT OUT

Direct students to check their work carefully. A first draft is rarely excellent. Encourage them to comb through their written work to ensure it contains the key components – for example, CORTED or TAILORED, verb endings, spellings, accents and punctuation. For even better accuracy, advise them to choose one aspect and go through the piece checking for just that. They should then return to the beginning and select another component to check.

49. HIGHLIGHTER CHALLENGE

When marking and giving feedback, don't correct every single error; instead, highlight the errors and hand back the written pieces to the learners. During a DIRT session, ask them to work out why you have highlighted something and to correct their own mistakes. Common misconceptions and errors can be discussed in pairs or as a class. Learners need to be able to spot and rectify their own mistakes, so this is a useful task to get them focused. Discussing and explaining why errors are errors can be a great starter task because the students have to recall previously learned grammar and phrases, which will help them to develop their thinking and improve their accuracy.

50. GRAMMAR CHECK

Expect students to check their grammatical structures explicitly. They don't always do this autonomously, so direct students to check key grammatical phrases and tenses to improve their accuracy. Model this to improve their confidence and precision. Students should be encouraged to check verb endings, the link between personal pronouns and the subject of the sentence, vowel rules and accents. In the run-up to writing assessments, I often ask my students to underline grammatical structures so I know they have checked them. This is excellent practice: not only are they scanning their work for generic errors but they are also focusing on tense usage. This strategy can aid in spoken work too. Attention to grammatical detail is important and this strategy ensures that the necessary checks happen.

I adore grammar – without it we can't construct beautiful poetry, prose or stories (and definitely not long paper chain sentences!). We have to teach our students grammar and they have to be able to use it competently and confidently. I am a builder of grammar: I teach scintillating phrases in the conditional mood alongside present tense opinion phrases. I do this so that my learners can say and write more. We create some 'best sentences' which reinforces these new phrases and encourages the learners to use them in their own work over time.

Learning grammar in this way is fun and exciting. Although crafting interesting and inventive sentences can be challenging, the students respond well to it. Some require support and scaffolding, so I always ensure that the structures I use are appropriate and that there are a range of examples. For example, I use a series of knowledge organisers to remind and help students to recall and identify grammar. I expect my students to learn and use grammar correctly; it is vital if they are to develop their language skills and avoid ambiguity.

In order to communicate in an original way they have to be able to use a range of tenses, so (depending on stage) they should be able to use more than one tense. I expect them to use two tenses with confidence (in spoken and written work) by the end of Year 7, then a third tense early in Year 8. The fourth, fifth and sixth then follow on. Students need to be able to understand tenses in their first language; when this knowledge is poor, the grammar work we do with them in the MFL classroom is even more important. When languages colleagues introduce tenses into their work in primary school, their young learners begin to understand, identify and use tenses correctly, so we should expect the same at secondary level. Expectations are everything; if we do not remind learners of grammar points in their first language, they can easily become confused.

I teach grammar in steps because I think it is easier to remember, and I also use song (especially 'The Pink Panther Theme' thanks to Helen Myers and Rachel Hawkes).[19] Learners love it and the rhythm aids memorisation. If I have taught it, I expect the students to know it and use it, and they do.

There are many discussions as to whether we should teach the whole paradigm. I do, because I don't want grammar to be a barrier to my learners' success. If they know the paradigm, they will recognise it and not fear it. Others prefer to teach partial elements of the paradigm, and that is

---

19 H. Myers, French: Avoir, to Have - Present Tense (10 February 2013) [video]. Available at: https://www.youtube.com/watch?v=3kWwS1_Kark.

their choice as professionals; we do what is best for the learners in front of us. Some educationalists observe that cognitive load might be an issue if we teach the whole paradigm, but I am of the opinion that it won't hamper them in assessments. I want my learners to check that their grammar is correctly formed in their written work, perhaps using time phrases (as extra detail) to embellish their work. If they can write it, they can speak it, and vice versa, so I also have high expectations for the correct use of spoken grammar.

Students need support with grammar; we differentiate with other aspects of learning and so we should with grammar. However, grammar is key and it must be mastered. With repeat exposure, recall and reminders they will get there. We know they will because we did too. Some teachers like to chunk phrases to make them easier for learners to memorise, and that is fine, providing they can manipulate grammar and use it appropriately. We should not expect grammar prowess without explicitly teaching it.

The language we use can sometimes be a barrier that we inadvertently build in when teaching grammar, so be mindful of the language you use. For many years I have used the phrase 'fun with grammar'. It makes my colleagues laugh, but I don't want my learners to perceive it as scary or impenetrable, so I make sure I don't teach it in that way. Grammar is very malleable: we can look at it, break it down and rebuild it, just like building blocks.

Make sure to add grammar checking to your checklists and criteria for success, and clearly state how many tenses you are expecting to see when setting tasks (both writing and speaking) and what these might be. When creating models or drawing responses from learners, remind them of any relevant grammatical aspects and ensure they know that grammar can be mastered.

CHAPTER 4

READING

FUN WITH READING IN THE MFL CLASSROOM

Developing reading skills in MFL at secondary level is made much easier thanks to primary colleagues, parents and carers, English teachers, tutors and other significant adults who read aloud to, read with and encourage young people to read independently. Engaging with books and printed literature is increasing (as is reading online).[1] There is a drive from schools to increase literacy levels and an enjoyment of reading, and charities like the National Literacy Trust are working to improve the accessibility of reading materials and books to young people.

The purpose of reading an international language text is to be exposed to authentic writing, new language and unfamiliar grammar constructions and to try to understand more than just the gist. It is often frustrating for learners who are confident readers in their native language, as they are used to understanding every word, skimming passages to identify the main themes and scanning for specific facts and details. Experiencing struggle when accessing international language texts may come as a shock which can overwhelm some learners and result in dissatisfaction. Sometimes the level of the text may not be

---

1   See, for example, C. Clark and A. Teravainen, Celebrating Reading for Enjoyment: Findings from our Annual Literacy Survey 2016 (London: National Literacy Trust, 2017). Available at: https://literacytrust.org.uk/research-services/research-reports/celebrating-reading-enjoyment-findings-our-annual-literacy-survey-2016-report.

age appropriate. It is a delicate balance: we do not want to besiege learners with complex texts, but equally we want to make it worth their while to read them.

As we saw in Chapter 3, teaching phonics is vital, not least because it allows students to break down unfamiliar words. By correlating the sound of the word with familiar words in English, learners can begin to dissect the language and gain an understanding of the text (as long as they are aware of false friends and red herrings).[2] Preparing students to tackle the literary texts and translations that have been added to the GCSE syllabus in recent years is an additional challenge, but it is not an unsurmountable one. Developing an understanding of how language works and is formed is essential, and this is gained through exposure to a range of authentic texts. Coupled with this is the challenge of finding high-quality texts which students can access but which are not belittling or childish. I have seen brilliant work in primary and secondary schools where learners have been culturally enriched as well as challenged through working with high-quality literary texts. In my experience, learners overcome their fear of the 'randomness' of some of the content and give it their best shot, which is excellent preparation for success in terminal assessments.

Reading aloud as a group, as part of a game or silently in assessment conditions can be a rewarding experience, *if* we teach learners how to read international language texts. Firstly, we need to explain that initially they won't know the meaning of every single word in the text, and that this is to be expected. Ensure they understand that when reading a text they should look for signposts (e.g. tense, time-frame, timeline) which will help them to

---

2   A false friend is a word that is often confused with a word in another language which actually has a different meaning because the two words look or sound similar.

gauge the topic and gist of the passage. They should try to identify any information they already know using CORTED or TAILORED (see Chapter 3), which will provide additional guidance as to the meaning of other phrases and sentences. The ability to recognise at least some items in the text can boost the students' confidence and help them to recall previously learned language. In turn, this will give them further options for seeking out answers and increasing their understanding of the text.

After reading through the text aloud, with the students following, I advise them to reread it individually at their own pace to get a feel for the passage – I call it 'warming up their brains' to the text. The learners will already be able to identify some familiar language, but on a second reading they should be able to glean more information about the content and context. Repeated readings should enable increasingly deeper access, especially for problematic words or phrases.

One of my colleagues encourages her students to underline the language they know. This provides a visual boost, increasing learners' confidence and keeping mindsets positive. Her view is that everyone can identify at least some language within a text. Her positive approach enables the learners to have a go, and it is exceedingly rare that a student can only recognise a single word. Interestingly, she also uses the centre pages of exercise books as a 'treasure chest' for learners to note down new and interesting vocabulary, chunks and phrases.

When setting a reading comprehension task, I challenge my learners to gather as much information as they can within the first two minutes. It is interesting how some just panic, some only read the first few lines and others read the title and then the questions. Whether it is an exam, test or class activity, I want them to read the questions first; this provides much-needed information about character, place, time-frame and activities. This context provides crucial detail for accessing, comprehending and deconstructing the text, which enables them to produce richer and more accurate responses – and, if that is the aim, gain more marks.

A reader's background knowledge of a topic can certainly enhance their understanding, but we also need to encourage students to make 'educated guesses' in the event that they don't know certain words or phrases, inferring meaning from the sentence and context of the passage, as well as recognising that repetition of a word or phrase suggests that it is important. This goes hand in hand with teaching students to identify cognates, partial cognates and false friends. Subheadings and images may also provide additional textual clues.

When reading a new text, the students tend to want to quickly skim it initially, scanning for words they know. This habit is a result of reading proficiency in their first language, and it can be harnessed to improve their reading of texts in other languages, so we should be encouraging skimming in the MFL classroom.

If you are struggling for time and need some reading texts, ask the students to create some best sentences using a collection of graphemes (maybe three). This can be set as a homework or an in-class activity. Collate and correct the sentences and use them as starters or tongue-twisters. This is a brilliant way to collect some wonderful texts that can be read aloud by the class. The learners experience a wonderful rush of joy when they realise that you are using their carefully crafted sentence, which helps to boost confidence and engagement, and you have a brilliant bank of tongue-twisters which can double up as translation or dictation tasks.

FIFTEEN TIPS FOR IMPROVING READING SKILLS IN THE MFL CLASSROOM

1   Encourage students to read the text through carefully using a ruler or bookmark.

2   On a second reading, allow students to highlight or underline the language they know using CORTED or TAILORED (see Chapter 3).

3   Ask the students to contextualise the text from the title, subheading, images and any questions.

4   If there are any reading comprehension questions, encourage the students to look through these before reading the text to provide some context.

5   If there are multiple questions, encourage the students to reread any comprehension questions related to the specific text so they are at the forefront of their minds when they are reading through. Too many times students don't do this and make careless errors.

6   If there aren't any questions, get the students to identify who, what, when, where and why (including opinions).

7   Remind the students to underline or highlight the answers they have found in the text, making a note of the answer number/letter to help them confirm their answers later.

8   Advise the students to check that their answers are in the language requested in the rubric.

9   They should also check that the question has been answered fully.

10 In some tests, the questions are asked in the order that the information appears in the text (although this should never be assumed). If they are stuck on an answer, advise the students to seek it out using this as a possible theory.

11 Encourage the learners to look out for signposts to help them (e.g. time indicators).

12 Prompt learners not to be tripped up by negatives, tenses, time indicators, false friends and red herrings. They could be and are likely to be present.

13 If a word is unknown, tell the learners not to panic; encourage them to decode the word through context and the language around it.

14 Remind students of the obvious: it's OK not to know every word and phrase. It can often be worked out.

15 Encourage the learners to do their best and never to leave a blank space or question unanswered. Urge them to make an educated guess.

READING, STORYTELLING AND SPEAKING

Although we know that students love being read to, using storytelling in languages lessons can seem like a luxury that time does not permit. However, the psychological, social and emotional benefits of being read to and reading aloud are obvious, and include bringing the language alive and helping learners to make links with their own lives and circumstances. It also boosts recall from long-term memory.

Students also benefit greatly from the opportunity to be creative with language, exercising their imagination through the language they know as well as embracing new and interesting vocabulary. Story writing takes planning and preparation, so they get to practise key skills used not only in languages but across a range of curriculum subjects. Writing a story but also sharing it orally – whether describing their culture, traditions, life experiences or opinions – provides a genuine purpose for developing oracy.

Telling a story can be emotive, exciting, passionate, intriguing and adventurous, all of which has to be conveyed clearly through the use of voice. Whether performing or listening, the Japanese visual art of storytelling, kamishibai, can deliver some memorable moments in language lessons (for more on this see Chapter 6). Students who are not natural performers enjoy being hidden from view during the performance, while others like to stand alongside the moving images as the story unfolds. Spending time on developing creativity can be challenging when contact time is reduced, flight paths[3] are calling and there is an assessment on the horizon. But if we want our students to be spontaneous with their language, then they need some time to develop this. Asking students to tell a story orally or through written work may enable them to explore language options previously precluded from them; the development of these skills may open their minds to the transference of grammar and vocabulary. If practised frequently – with support and guidance – creative work can help with recall, confidence, fluency,

---

3   A flight path maps the linear trajectory of a learner's expected progress throughout secondary education. Learners' achievements are tracked and monitored against these maps.

spontaneity and oracy, all of which are prized well beyond the MFL classroom and terminal assessments.

CHAPTER 5

LISTENING

If there is one language skill in which students tend to feel least experienced, it's listening. Yet it is the first skill that humans are able to perform – according to Professor Sophie Scott, we start listening at 24 weeks as developing foetuses.[1] That's right, we can hear before we are born, listening to voices and sounds in utero. Dr Fabrice Wallois and colleagues have established that 'shortly after birth, human infants already exhibit a variety of sophisticated linguistic capacities' and are able to discriminate between syllables and human language.[2]

I asked my learners why listening exam tasks were such a challenge for them, and these are some of the reasons they gave:

- The speech is so fast.

- It doesn't seem like natural speech.

- It sounds weird.

- It's too slow in places.

- There is too much to do.

- The recording doesn't give you long enough to think it through. You hear it in [language] and have to read

---

1   Reported in M. Roberts, Babies Can Hear Syllables in the Womb, Says Research, *BBC News* (26 February 2013). Available at: https://www.bbc.co.uk/news/health-21572520.

2   M. Mahmoudzadeh, G. Dehaene-Lambertz, M. Fournier, G. Kongolo, S. Goudjil, J. Dubois, R. Grebe and F. Wallois, Syllabic Discrimination in Premature Human Infants Prior to Complete Formation of Cortical Layers, *Proceedings of the National Academy of Sciences of the United States of America* 110(12) (2013): 4846-4851 at 4846. Available at: https://www.pnas.org/content/110/12/4846.

the question-and-answer options which are in [language]. Then, before you finish reading the options, while replaying the sounds in your head and not saying it out loud (in case you get into trouble from examiners/teachers or distract other people around you), you hear it again and it puts you off.

● Can it be played more than twice?

● The beep is off-putting.

● In conversation, if you are unclear on what was said, you ask for clarification and the language used is varied or changes, but in a listening activity they repeat the same phrase, which isn't natural.

● They say all of the options so it's really hard to keep the information in your head while reading the text.

● I try to work out an answer, but I need more time to hear it. Give me more time and control of the recording and I'll get there.

● Can't you read it, Miss, or one of the other languages teachers? Your voices are familiar.[3]

● How can you work it out in two seconds? Every other exam gives you way more time to work out the answer.

● It's so much harder than the other listening tasks we do.

---

3 A colleague who has extensive experience working with students with hearing impairments has observed that they have 'no chance' with a recording because they use lip patterns and facial expressions to 'hear'. This is obviously not possible with a recording. A live speaker would be preferable in these circumstances, and perhaps for all learners.

● Can it be like This Is Language so that it can be slowed down?[4]

Their feelings are based on experience, a point which is reinforced by Robert Vanderplank.[5] Unfortunately, they are also enhanced by fear, which is why one of my duties as their teacher is to ensure that they are taught how to listen and what this means when attending to and deciphering an international language. As native English speakers, learners often forget what they do when they listen because it happens so naturally. Therefore, it is important that learners know how to listen, so they can overcome their anxieties and have a real chance of decoding the language they hear. Done well, listening exercises can feel like a game and are nothing to be afraid of. In this way, learners understand the message being conveyed with increased confidence and clarity.

Of course, students' mindsets affect their approach to, and success at, listening tasks, which is compounded by a lack of positive listening experiences and by underdeveloped listening skills. All three factors are clearly in play in the comments from my students. Learners' perception that listening is incomprehensible and 'too hard' results in paralysis for some, while others start looking around the room and seeking reinforcement from their peers instead of focusing on the language and working out their response.

Too often, listening skills aren't taught because teachers assume that all learners can listen. They know how to do this in their first language, so surely they can listen in the

---

4 This Is Language produce audio-visual materials, games and interactive exercises for use in the MFL classroom. See wwwthisislanguage.com.

5 R. Vanderplank, Listening and Understanding. In P. Driscoll, E. Macaro and A. Swarbrick (eds), *Debates in Modern Languages Education* (Abingdon and New York: Routledge, 2014), pp. 53–65.

international language too. In practice this may not be true (check recent test scores for listening against performance in the other language skills if you need confirmation). Each language skill must be taught. When done well, the learners begin to feel an increased sense of self-confidence and self-efficacy, and start to believe that success in listening exercises is realistic and attainable. Of course, if we fail to prepare them for the reality, then they won't achieve as well as they might.

As teachers, we need to ensure that we are challenging learners' perceptions of listening. We must address this head-on by challenging our own behaviour and language when setting up a task. I have been in the privileged position of observing teachers, and it is interesting to see that the verbal instructions for listening exercises are often undermined by negative connotations. This can occur in language (for example, 'I know you don't like this' or 'I know you find it challenging') and body language (especially facial expressions – I have even seen grimacing!), all without the teacher realising it is happening.

Teachers often don't appreciate that their own perception of how difficult listening can be is communicated to their students, resulting in the negativity we tend to see towards it. We need to set up listening exercises with success in mind and show the learners in our classrooms that these are not insurmountable tasks. Self-efficacy and a can-do approach is as important as the belief that they will complete the task and do it well. We have to adopt a more positive approach to setting up listening tasks. We need to show learners what we expect, and how to get there, through good classroom modelling. We need to guide them step by step to ensure that we don't make listening the least favoured skill of language learning. Motivation to succeed should be high but it is not the only factor. The ability to recognise chunks of grammar and vocabulary items is important, but so is the capacity to use them correctly and effectively to complete the comprehension tasks that inevitably accompany the listening task in an assessment.

One of the problems with learning a language in the UK is that it is deemed to be 'harshly graded' at GCSE and A level, resulting in the perception that higher grades can only be attained by native speakers. Many students vote with their feet and opt for subjects in which they feel they can attain more easily. How do we counter this mindset? We have to ensure that we are mindful of our language and that senior leadership team (SLT) members and pastoral leaders do not do our subjects a disservice by making languages seem unattractive and inaccessible. We need to make sure that our curriculum enables learners to use the language across all four language skills, and access materials that are more in line with their age and interests, thus making the content more conversational and mature. We also need to ensure that we give our learners access to a languages experience which enables them to communicate with confidence with their international peers and to not be afraid of this. They must believe that they can do it, that we are enabling them to do it and that the language comes alive when they do so. Communication is key but it need not mean 100% accuracy. Finally, students must believe in our confidence in their ability – this should be absolute and non-negotiable.

A lack of appropriate listening materials is mentioned repeatedly by languages teachers in schools, despite listening activities appearing in most language textbooks. However, our learners must rise to the challenge of being confident listeners, so we have to find a way to teach them which is accessible to all. Listening to and understanding language is an active, cognitive translation process which requires formal teaching and support. Breaking down the listening process and developing the essential aspects of it will develop learners' listening skills and confidence. Taught alongside phonics it can improve student outcomes, as their knowledge of phonemes helps them to recognise words and in turn answer the questions that have been set. Equally, warming up learners' ears by giving them pre-listening tasks which enable them to hear the language being spoken can help students to make the transition between their native language and the international language.

In his research, Ekrem Solak has identified the 'listening sub-skills' most frequently used in the MFL classroom:[6]

- Listening for gist – listening for broad ideas but not detailed understanding.

- Listening for specific information – listening for a particular piece of information.

- Listening in detail – listening to understand as many details as possible.

- Listening to infer – listening to understand feelings and make inferences.

- Listening to questions and responding – listening in order to answer questions.

- Listening to description – listening to the detail in a description.

By teaching these six different aspects of listening we can help learners to become more confident when completing listening tasks. However, we should not underestimate the increased cognitive comprehension that comes from

---

6   E. Solak, Teaching Listening Skills. In E. Solak (ed.), *Teaching Language Skills for Prospective English Teachers* (Istanbul: Pelikan, 2016), pp. 29–44 at p. 35. Available at: https://www.researchgate.net/publication/309293240_Teaching_ Listening_Skills.

knowing and being confident in the phoneme–grapheme link.

Whatever the level they are at, it is helpful for students to have the questions in front of them when they are listening. These will give them a sense of the different aspects of the audio clip they are about to hear. If there is reading time or a short pause before the recording begins, encourage the students to read the questions and hypothesise about the language they might hear. Again, this serves to warm up the brain and aids with comprehension. Learners should be encouraged to really focus on the questions while completing the listening task. Their brains are working to identify the words, phrases and grammar, translate these into their native language, read the text (which might be in a grid format) or multiple-choice questions, look at the images and identify true/false or not mentioned items, as well as considering the time-frame. There is a significant amount to do, all in a matter of seconds.

I often play foreign news bulletins in the classroom (without the visuals, so the students only have to focus on the sound). I will play it three or four times to help them develop their aural proficiency in listening to a range of native speakers talking fluently and at speed. This practice supports the students to identify overarching topics, vocabulary and grammar in context, as well as learning to listen to a second language without reverting to their 'native brain'. By this I mean that learners need to develop the skill of listening to language spoken by people who are not their teacher and automatically applying the international language phonemes they have learned. This will enable them to more easily identify the language and grammar used, and therefore understand the context.

It is clear from studying many examiners' reports that learners often use native language phonemes in stressful situations. To best serve our learners, we have to ensure that their brains can automatically switch from native language to international language. This takes practice, patience and time, but it will result in more successful listening experiences. Once this skill has been developed, the learners will be more confident and far less negative when it comes to listening exercises, especially in the terminal exams at GCSE and A level.

We should of course teach our learners to understand more than the gist. However, when they are first developing their language skills listening for gist can provide a good foundation and, in time, knowledge, understanding and application of the grapheme–phoneme link. Gist is especially useful when learners are completing listening tasks because it helps them to break down a long string of language and identify any words they know. As students develop this skill and amass more positive experiences, the negative mindset we identified earlier slowly changes. This will not happen overnight: it will take repeated exposure to a range of listening tasks over a sustained period of time to shift ingrained ways of thinking.

I know of schools where listening has been a key focus for a number of years in order to address the problem of poor scores in the GCSE listening exam. They have instituted a strategic plan to develop listening skills from Year 7 onwards to ensure that these are comparable with other stronger language skills. The strategy goes well beyond listening for gist and predicting which language may be heard. It incorporates Solak's six sub-skills, which reinforces the importance of listening, but also develops learners' self-confidence and self-belief that listening is an achievable task. As with any development, close monitoring and tracking, as well as good-quality feedback, are required to ensure that learners not only experience success but also know what to do to reach the next echelon.

TRANSCRIPTS AND SUBTITLES

Transcripts can help learners to make the link between spoken and written language. Transcript activities give students the opportunity to identify words they know visually, which can help to decrease stress and cognitive load. It takes time for learners to improve their ability to retain oral language heard during a listening activity, but this skill will help them to identify individual words and grammatical phrases, and not just hear a long string of spoken language. Obviously, transcripts are not allowed in formal assessments, but in the classroom they can be excellent for boosting learners' aptitude in accessing language and identifying familiar elements. In my experience, students are more likely to take a risk and make a logical guess at an unfamiliar word or phrase if they have understood some of the other vocabulary and grammar.

News clips, TV programmes and films are an underused resource in the languages classroom, but they offer a superb way of developing students' listening confidence. Vanderplank suggests that subtitles can have a transformative impact on learners because they make the language more accessible and enjoyable.[7] Think about the last time you watched an international film in a language which is not your strength. As your ears warmed up to the language, you gradually 'got it' and became more fluent and able to understand it. However, if you were to watch the same film with subtitles, you would achieve that level of success much sooner. The brain is connecting the graphemes and phonemes together, making the flow of language more accessible and meaningful.

---

7   Vanderplank, Listening and Understanding.

DICTATION

Dictation has become de rigueur in the languages classroom once again as an increased focus and importance is placed on listening. Students can grow to enjoy dictation tasks, especially if the exercise is repeated and gains are made in word and phrase identification. By practising dictation with a range of teachers' voices students' confidence can rise exponentially, leading to improvements in listening task completion. Try using digital devices to pre-record dictation to add variety to learners' listening experiences, and share these with colleagues across the MFL team. The recordings can be used as individual listening tasks to be transcribed or translated, so you have created a resource with multiple applications.

TWELVE TIPS FOR IMPROVING LISTENING SKILLS IN THE MFL CLASSROOM

1   Teach students the phonics grapheme–phoneme link.

2   Teach students Solak's six sub-skills of listening – one at a time over time.

3   Do not rely solely on textbook listening exercises.

4   Create a bank of authentic listening exercises. These can be captured from TV, podcasts, radio and the internet. Clips can be found on TV channel and magazine websites and are usually freely available for use. They might need to be adapted by creating a transcript or subtitles to aid access.

5   Create a bank of listening exercises for your classes, which can also double up as pre-listening warm-up tasks. These should different to the authentic listening exercises described in the previous point.

6   Recycle and reuse the listening tasks in order to develop the six sub-skills.

7   Expose learners to a range of voices when completing listening tasks.

8   Give students listening homework tasks.

9   Use dictation in class as a powerful listening activity.

10 Interleave listening activities throughout every lesson and every topic.

11 Create listening activities which build skill through the identified six sub-skills of listening.

12 Always be positive about listening tasks, activities and exercises.

And repeat. I say that because, overwhelmingly, listening is the skill that some students dread the most. Building competence in listening starts with the elements discussed above, as well as frequent exposure to different voices across a range of listening tasks. The more learners are exposed to listening – with the expectation that they can do it and will become more successful at it – the more mindsets will change, and in time it will no longer be feared.

Your listening tasks shouldn't play second fiddle to writing tasks, not least because listening is the first skill we acquire as humans. Listening must be a serious focus in the classroom because it has such a significant impact on other language learning skills. I am sure that with increased exposure all four language skills – listening, speaking, reading and writing – will be strengthened and learners will achieve success. This takes time, so it is best to start in Year 7 (or earlier if you are in an all-through-school). Students can hear and listen proficiently in their first language, so there is no reason why this can't be achieved in the MFL classroom.

CHAPTER 6

CREATIVITY IN MFL

I truly believe that creativity has a significant role to play in language learning. Encouraging students to be creative makes language experiences seem more memorable and alive, as students are enabled to use language in a personal way. In most subjects at school, I remember being directed to sit at a desk and work through a textbook, but in the languages classroom we were expected to use a variety of strategies to practise the language we were learning – whether for end-of-year assessments, GCSE or A level – which seemed very novel at the time. It has been my experience that ditching the textbook and allowing young people to use language imaginatively has a hugely positive impact, so this chapter contains some of my favourite creative solutions.

DRAMA IN MFL

SOCK PUPPETS

Sock puppets are widely available but are often expensive. Encouraging your students to be creative and expressive by making their own puppets can open up a brilliantly imaginative languages experience. With some inexpensive stationery and craft items (all good supermarkets have a stationery/craft aisle), as well as multipacks of plain white or interestingly patterned/coloured socks, creative magical moments can happen in the MFL classroom. Issue instructions in the target language about how to construct a sock puppet, model this for them, dual code it in the international language and set them off, allowing them to communicate in the target language only. The students will remember the lesson and, I promise, the sock puppets will be a topic of discussion for years to come.

Completed sock puppets can be used in future lessons to encourage spoken work. The students often don't realise they are learning, recalling key language and reinforcing key linguistic structures when devising adventures for their sock puppets, creating role plays or short presentations, or answering questions. But one thing is certain: they raise their game. This has a positive impact on pronunciation, tone and projection, which are all important in developing confident orators.

Sock puppets can provide social and emotional support to students who don't want the focus to be on them; instead the audience's attention is directed at the puppet. Using a desk or classroom door as a 'theatre' can entice even the most reticent of speakers to speak up. The student can hide behind the 'stage' and is free to create interesting and comedic voices using captivating and powerful language. Performances of this type also assist anxious students to work with one another, developing turn-taking as well as creating, designing and managing second-language interactions.

FANCY DRESS BOX

As with sock puppets, a fancy dress box is a boon in the MFL classroom. A dressing-up box full of colour and texture can create intrigue and excitement. Throughout my experience of MFL teaching, the power of the fancy dress box has been phenomenally positive for reticent or challenging students. The power of a rainbow clown wig is something to behold! However, whether it is a mysterious Venetian masquerade mask, giant novelty sunglasses, sombrero, pirate eyepatch or mousquetaire cavalier-style feathered hat, the dressing-up box allows students to become someone else. By harnessing their inner creative nature and channelling this through their spoken language, a fun classroom activity or assessment can become a serious performance, in which linguistic competence is demonstrated through delightful grammatical choices as well as a depth and range of vocabulary.

Students usually want their performances to be amusing and memorable (for the right reasons), but also for their effort and hard work to be acknowledged. We should encourage their oral performances to be well designed, to show language progression by using impressive structures, grammar, vocabulary and register, to be clear in their pronunciation and project their voice well, and to demonstrate good body language through their stance, posture and use of space.

The dressing-up box can be used on lots of occasions in the MFL classroom to ease anxiety, boost confidence and nurture a growing confidence in your young orators' second language. As with sock puppets, the students often don't even realise they are learning and developing their linguistic skills; they just know they are having fun. Positive memories create deeper learning experiences which help students to recall the language they need more readily. Interestingly, when preparing for speaking assessments or peer-assessed tasks, students like to bring in an item or two of their own to assist in their performance. I find that it helps to significantly increase their enthusiasm and engagement, being an emotional prop for some and something they use in the performance for others. I expect my students to take their spoken work – with or without performance-enhancing items – seriously, and they are very aware of this.

DRAMA

The power of drama in MFL is not to be underestimated. Students' linguistic skills and creativity are challenged, and wonderful stories can unfold from set tasks or loose guidance. Giving students a starting point – a headline for their focus – allows them to use language to create something fresh and exciting. Drama can be a powerful motivator, encouraging hungry minds to seek out new and interesting vocabulary and constructions. It takes learners away from their desks and enables them to bring their inner creative selves to the fore.

For some this will be a welcome change, but for others it might be terrifying, so it is important to know your class well. Provide differentiated structures or tasks for those who might require it so they can get the most out of breaking out from behind their desks. Many learners enjoy drama once they have warmed up to the idea of performing a piece of language work in front of their peers. Recording their performance on a digital device, to be watched and appreciated in a future lesson, may help to encourage full participation by anxious artistes.

STORYTELLING

Storytelling is an underused medium in MFL. A degree of free rein to tell a story from their own perspective – coupled with the bonus of getting out from behind desks and off chairs and into an open space with a wealth of items to inspire their creative appetites – invariably enhances learners' linguistic pieces, whether they are monologues or collaborative compositions. Students sharing their own stories through the medium of drama in the target language is wonderful and a magical moment in the MFL classroom.

Over the years I have collected a range of books for students to read, look at and enjoy both inside and outside the classroom. Some learners have been inspired by these books when creating their own stories, but I also recall a Key Stage 4 class asking to read one of my more challenging books because they missed reading for pleasure – something they had enjoyed at Key Stage 3. We selected a book and then set about reading it aloud across multiple lessons (this took place over a three-week period as the book wasn't our primary focus). The students loved the ritual of putting their work aside and uncovering their storybooks. Calm and focus descended the room as they began to recall the story so far, with their enthusiasm and engagement increasing as we discussed the fates of the characters and tried to ascertain what would happen next.

We also used the text for some translation tasks, plus the students noted unfamiliar vocabulary and grammar items and then spent time trying to weave these into their written and spoken work. Not only did the learners find this activity relaxing, but it also provided them with additional opportunities to study literary texts. To them this was time out; they didn't appreciate that we were studying and analysing a literary text, unpicking it and manipulating the language, as well as learning new grammar and vocabulary – all skills required for the terminal assessment.

Finding literature that is appropriate can be time-consuming and buying books can be expensive, so storytelling may not seem like an obvious activity to turn to; however, it can be a fantastic way to engage students in reading. Discount bookshops can be a brilliant source for affordable reading materials, as are online bookstores which sell titles in a wide range of international languages.

KAMISHIBAI

Kamishibai, the ancient Japanese art of visual storytelling, is a wonderful way to weave stories into languages lessons. Kamishibai is a form of Japanese street theatre and story-telling. It originated in Buddhist temples in the 12th century. Monks enticed onlookers into hearing religious and moral stories at a time when illiteracy rates were high and books and reading materials were inaccessible for many people. Kamishibai filtered out into the streets of Japan, generating large audiences who loved hearing stories, whether or not they had a moral point. Performers travelled with a miniature stage set into which they inserted a series of illustrated boards, narrating the story by changing the images. Kamishibai became extremely popular during the post-war period and remained so until television became an affordable commodity during the 20th century.

Thankfully, kamishibai has found its way into the class-room. Students can be directed to create a short story individually or as a group piece using newly learned topic vocabulary, such as a daily routine or role play scenario. Students should identify eight (or more) key points within their stories and generate A3 images to reflect them. More confident artists may choose to draw or paint their illustra-tions, while others may prefer to create images using ICT. The story is recorded on the back of the paper sheets as a prompt, but some students challenge themselves to learn it by heart. The story does not have to be long: too long and it becomes challenging for students to learn, too short and it is hard to generate eight illustrative images.

Kamishibai is traditionally performed using a small wooden theatre, although it is possible to make one out of a cardboard box that's suitable for holding A3 paper. Set up your class theatre and invite the students to become storytellers for their classmates. The storytellers should be hidden by the theatre and move the images as the story unfolds. Taking on the role of storyteller can have a dramatic impact on students' oracy skills, including projection, tone and intonation.

Synching the storytelling with moving images requires practice, so make sure you give the students enough time to pull their performances together. Portraying their stories using beautiful and striking visuals, alongside a purposeful opportunity to create an interesting and entertaining language piece, provides learners with a deep learning experience. My students have shared some magical stories through the medium of kamishibai. If you have partner primaries or teach younger students, do share the joy of kamishibai with them too.

MUSIC IN MFL

Most people respond positively to music. I have seen it used superbly in non-music lessons to focus and aid the transition from one activity to the next. In the MFL classroom, some learners don't even notice that the songs they are hearing are in another language! Utterly aghast at this, it became my mission to awaken their auditory appreciation and develop their musical tastes by exposing them to French, German and Spanish music in lessons as part of a music project.

We started with an assembly which included international language music to whet the students' appetites for a week of activities to celebrate and promote languages from many cultures. The students loved it. Many of them were unaware of how international composers and artists had already touched their lives – from musical mobiles to aid sleep when they were infants through to nursery rhymes, TV advertisements and films. They enjoyed researching international artists and presenting their work to the class, sharing their new love of French rap, German metal and Spanish pop. Many wanted these newly unearthed songs as ringtones, and frequently came to find the languages team to share the latest track from Diam's, Nâdiya, Mylène Farmer or Stromae. It made for interesting and engaging times!

We were fortunate to have two FLAs (the school offered three international languages), so we enlisted their help in the project too. They worked hard to collate a range of songs, as well as details of (appropriate) websites and fan sites that voracious linguists could explore to gain more musical inspiration about groups, artists and genres. They also suggested reading materials, such as magazine articles and journals, in addition to the fantastically rich language which appears in song lyrics.

We also had support from the music department, plus the use of their amazing suite of rooms and instruments at breaktimes and lunchtimes. The end goal of the project was for the learners to create their own songs, raps and performances in French, German and Spanish – and they didn't disappoint. The motivation and engagement, both in groups and individually, was high. The songs and performances were sensational and enjoyed by all. The marriage of creativity and musical talent with dance routines and professionalism was breathtaking. It was one of those magical moments in my teaching career that I won't forget. The project was memorable for the learners too. They weren't just learning a second language; they were singers and musicians fulfilling a dream of writing a song and having an eager audience for whom they could perform their work.

There are songs, and then there are songs. 'Despacito', 'Aserejé', '99 Luftballons' and 'Joe Le Taxi' are renowned as international music, but they aren't representative of the amazing array that's out there. We can do so much more than simply play Serge Gainsbourg, Plastic Bertrand and Téléphone and suggest that it represents French music; equally with Nena, Conchita Wurst and Rammstein for German music, and Shakira, Enrique Iglesias, Justin Bieber, Luis Fonsi and Daddy Yankee for Spanish music. However, whether you like them or not, tracks by these musicians have made it into the UK charts. The learners know about them and often love them, sometimes knowing all the lyrics and the moves (yikes!). It is therefore a perfect opportunity to cement their linguistic skills, but also widen their musical and cultural knowledge by recommending other artists and genres.

My advice is to choose your artists and songs carefully. Just because you can understand the lyrics, doesn't mean the learners will too. Some songs have a political message or may contain inappropriate language, and lyrics can be misogynistic or over-sexualised for young ears. We must be mindful of this and not just opt for catchy or popular tunes. The learners are likely to seek out the video and words, so make sure you don't prompt irate parents to raise concerns. Safeguarding is paramount.

To really impact on learning, you also need to consider how you can use the song beyond just one lesson. If you don't, it will fizzle out like a wet firework instead of creating a memorable language enhancing experience. There are scintillating conversations to be had about language, culture and musical preferences following a musical discovery or recommendation. In the table that follows, I have listed some tracks that I have used over the years, that I've either stumbled across myself or that have been shared with me by FLAs or excited learners. Some of them are not my cup of tea, but it's all a musical education. At the start of the music project I always played 'Joe Le Taxi'. Despite disliking the song personally, the learners loved it, and it was simple and easy for them to learn. This meant that when it came to creating their own songs I could remind them of the simplicity of it. Songs can hook learners into new language, and some lyrics provide a perfect platform for listening exercises, warm-up pre-listening tasks, cloze exercises, grammar study and for stealing favourite lines or vocabulary items to introduce into written and spoken work, but also to enjoy and to promote discussion.

INTERNATIONAL MUSIC ARTISTS TO CREATE INTRIGUE IN THE MFL CLASSROOM

There are so many more – these don't even scratch the surface!

French	German	Spanish
Celine Dion	Alligatoah	Alaska
Chilla	Bushido	Bad Bunny
Christine and the Queens	Conchita Wurst	Buena Vista Social Club
Francis Cabrel	Dero Goi	Camila Cabello

French	German	Spanish
Indochine	Die Ärtze	Da Souza
Jacques Brel	Excuse Me Moses	Enrique Iglesias
Jonny Halliday	Falco	Fuel Fandango
Julien Doré	Herbert Grönemeyer	Jennifer Lopez
Les innocents	Kollegah	Julio Iglesias
Manu Chao	Kraftwerk	Las Ketchup
MC Solaar	Nena	Lori Meyers
Ménélik	Opus	Los Planetas
Mickey 3D	Paul van Dyk	Miami Sound Machine/Gloria Estefan
Mylène Farmer	Polarkreis 18	Nudozurdo
Nâdiya	Rammstein	Ricky Martin
Noir Désir	Sarah Connor	Rozalén
Peace and Loves	Scooter	Santana/Carlos Santana
Sniper	Tokio Hotel/Billy/Bill Kaulitz	Shakira
Stromae	Xavier Naidoo	Triángulo de Amor Bizarro
Zazie		

ART IN MFL

I have seen, heard and read about many brilliant examples of content and language integrated learning (CLIL)[1] introducing ambitious language projects in schools, where a strong link with the art department has had a huge impact on both art and languages. I recall a colleague from my own school sharing her love of Paul Klee with Key Stage 4 and 5 German learners to great effect. It was her passion for Klee's art that delighted the learners, enriching them with both cultural capital and more complex linguistic structures in her descriptions of the artist's work. These weren't the most able students, but this mini project and series of lessons really brought the German language alive. It was an unforgettable experience that they will treasure.

Find out if there is the potential for an enriching cross-curricular project in your school. If so, plan it carefully with a view to developing the learners' cultural and artistic understanding as well as their language skills. If a collaboration is not possible, there is a series of short films called *1 minute au musée*, which can help MFL teachers to weave art into language lessons and promote brilliant discussion.[2] There are around 140 episodes which follow three characters: Mona, Raphaël and Nabi. They visit museums to look at great works of art created by the world's most celebrated artists across a range of movements and periods. Mona, Raphaël and Nabi observe, study and unpick each artwork or artefact: key facts, dates and details are shared using a wealth of fast-paced vocabulary, all squeezed into 60 seconds.

---

1   The idea behind CLIL is to teach the subject and the language together, with the aim of enhancing the communication and language abilities of young people. For more on this see Chapter 9.

2   See https://education.francetv.fr/matiere/arts/ce1/serie/1-minute-au-musee.

The three amusing characters, along with their questions and hilarious comments about each work of art, instantly hook in the students. There are no subtitles, but the images and their knowledge from art lessons will help learners to decipher this information. Of course, it is important to consider the purpose of showing the film or programme and to plan careful scaffolding to ensure the students meet the learning goals. I have used them to improve learners' listening skills, but also to develop their cultural knowledge and understanding. Don't forget to warm up the learners' ears to the language first through pre-listening tasks.

FILM IN MFL

Film is very popular and a great medium for engaging learners. Viewing appropriate film and video clips can be a positive aural and visual experience in the languages class-room, and it often doesn't seem like learning. I remember challenging a group of students who struggled with lan-guages to watch a French film, *Les Choristes*. Many of them panicked initially, but by the end every single one of the learners was hooked – they loved it. It was a truly mem-orable learning experience, not least because it was the first time they had watched an international language film. When the learners finished Key Stage 4, they recalled watching this film as one of the 'magical moments' of their secondary schooling. Some even shared the film with their families and siblings, which still fills me with joy, even now.

I adore world cinema, and I want to be able to share this passion with my learners. But it isn't easy. One of the prob-lems is that UK film classification is very strict compared to mainland Europe, so finding appropriate international language films to watch with any class from Year 3 to Year 13 can be challenging.

When putting together an MFL film project in my school, the teachers first watched all the films to ensure that they were appropriate, engaging and relevant for our students. We then went on to create activities to support world cinema watching in our classrooms. The charity Into Film (which has given every school across the UK the chance to have their own film club) provides an impressive array of films and resource packs for schools, which allows teachers to use films to enrich topics, lessons and subjects. Into Film have curated a catalogue of over 3,000 films and resources, including world cinema films, which have been reviewed by teachers but more importantly have an age rating. It is well worth being a member – it is free to sign up for an account.[3]

LANGUAGE FILMS TO ENJOY WITH KEY STAGE 3

One of the bonuses of an MFL film project is that, although at the start the learners are fearful that they won't understand what is happening and won't be able to keep up with the dialogue, within a short period of time they do understand and want to watch more foreign language films. Initially, I tend to break the film up into episodes, so it is not too overwhelming. I also create booklets brimming with tasks, so they have to really engage with the film. Even the most reticent of language learners remember watching certain films and feel incredible success at watching an entire film in French, German or Spanish. This isn't about watching a movie to pass the time, but engaging learners with the fluency and flow of native speakers

---

3   See www.intofilm.org.

and the richness and range of the language used – plus the exotic locations and beautiful scenery which transport learners out of the classroom and into exciting foreign lands. I can't tell you how many learners have said, 'I didn't even know that they made [language] films, Miss!'

There are some weird and wonderful films listed in the table that follows. Always watch the film first to ensure that it is suitable, do your research and be ready to explain the link to the learning, not only to learners and their parents but also to other teachers and school leaders. Ask yourself the following questions:

- Is the film appropriate viewing for these young people? What themes do I need to be aware of?
- Why are they watching the film?
- What are they going to learn from it?
- How will this experience help them to develop their language skills and cultural understanding?
- What work with they have to complete alongside watching the film?

According to Into Film, the following films have an age rating of 11+. Some have a lower age rating of 7+, but the good news for MFL teachers is that they are all perfect for Key Stage 3.

Watching a film can be a real treat and a totally unforgettable experience for learners of any ability, mainstream or otherwise, providing you have carefully thought through the purpose and tasks you have planned to deliver alongside it, and providing appropriate scaffolding and support are in place for those who need it. Explore and unpick the films with your learners, and make sure they don't forget the experience in a hurry.

French	German	Spanish
À la folie, pas du tout	Cargo (2009)	Carlitos y el campo de los sueños
Astérix et Obélix	Die Abenteuer des Prinzen Achmed	El juego (2014)
Cyrano de Bergerac	Hamsa	Goal!
Ernest et Célestine	Joyeux Noël	Maktub (2011)
Jean de Florette and Manon des Sources	Max Minsky und ich	Metegol/The Unbeatables
Kirikou	Netto	Valentin
La gloire de mon père	Sophie Scholl: Die letzten Tage	Voces Innocentes
Le Grand Méchant Renard et autres contes	Suite Française	Wakolda
Le petit Nicholas	Wakolda	Zipi y Zape y el club de la canica
Les 400 Coups	Encounters Short Film Festival – a range of short films across several years many suitable for Key Stage 3 (just search for Encounters Short Film Festival on the Into Film website)	
Les Aventures extraordinaires d'Adèle Blanc-Sec		
Les Choristes		
Les Triplettes de Belleville		
Les Visiteurs		

Populaire

Ma vie de Courgette

Micmacs

Monsieur Lazhar

The Illusionist/L'Illusionniste

Un monstre à Paris

Une vie de chat

Yamakasi

FILMS FOR KEY STAGE 4 AND BEYOND

The following films provide more challenge and require more maturity, not least because some of the themes are more worldly and the language content more sophisticated. When preparing to watch any of these films with learners, I have sent a letter home to parents in advance, giving them an overview of the film, its certification and a link to the Into Film website, as well as informing them of some of the themes. Parents have thanked me for this information, and no complaints or concerns have been raised. It has been lovely to hear at parents' evenings that Key Stage 4 and 5 learners have gone home and watched the film again with their parents (with subtitles). The students have also organised film nights with friends to watch international language films as a result of an in-school MFL film experience.

French	German	Spanish
À bout de souffle	*Berlin 36*	*Abel*
Amélie	*Das Boot*	*El Espírito de la Colmena*
Bande de filles	*Die fetten Jahre sind vorbei/The Edukators*	*El laberinto del fauno/Pan's Labyrinth*
Entre les murs/ The Class	*Das Leben der Anderen*	*El Olivo*
Paris, je t'aime	*Die Welle*	*La jaula de oro*
La Vie en rose	*Good Bye, Lenin!*	*Todo sobre mi madre*
La Haine	*Lola rennt/Run Lola Run*	*Volver*
Ma vie en rose	*Styx* (2018)	

For those of you wondering what fresh and different theme to embrace to celebrate European Day of Languages in September, Into Film have put together lists of films (11 suitable for primary learners and 22 for different stages within secondary).[4] You can use these to support language learning and to develop cultural knowledge and understanding, as well as to celebrate French, German and Spanish cinema. For more details check out the lists for yourselves and enjoy.

---

4   See https://www.intofilm.org/films/filmlist/31.

CHAPTER 7

THE AWESOME POWER OF LUCKY SOCKS

FUN WITH ASSESSMENT

Many students don't like tests and assessments, but for some learners it goes beyond mere dislike. Assessments and end-of-unit/topic/year tests elicit feelings of fear, worry and failure. Low-stakes testing was set to put paid to these concerns, but as an anxious test performer myself I felt there was more that could be done.

As a department, we had already demystified the assessment criteria, the students knew what a great one looks like through modelling and feedback, and they understood the next steps they had to take to improve, develop and enrich their work. Creativity has always been an attribute in my MFL classroom, so I naturally started to look for ways to make testing creative. Of course, students need to complete their assessments, but there are ways to do this that do not lead to high levels of anxiety and stress, so *creative assessment* became a feature in my classroom.

TWENTY CREATIVE ALTERNATIVES TO TRADITIONAL ASSESSMENT

These are my favourite creative assessment activities which enable students to feel relaxed enough to really show me what they know:

1   Knowledge poster/knowledge burst – students have an allocated amount of time to put down everything they know about a specific unit, topic or aspect of the subject. This does not have to be in prose.

2   Mind map of vocabulary on a certain topic.

3   Lists of key vocabulary or grammatical phrases – allocate a certain amount of time for this.

4   Quizzes – allocate a certain amount of time and ask the students to create a quiz which can serve as a form of assessment for their peers. They should also create an answer sheet.

5   Two truths, one lie (see Chapter 3).

6   Thirty circles – the students have an allocated amount of time to complete their thirty circles sheet (see page 151) with key vocabulary, knowledge or language they have been expected to learn.

7   Best sentence (see Chapter 3).

8   Best paragraph (see Chapter 3).

9   Rally Robin (see Chapter 3).

10 Act out – give students a word, phrase, sentence or piece of text and ask them to act it out. Make sure you give them time to translate it first and be clear

whether you would like them to act it out in the international language or in English. This is always great fun in groups.

11 Create a game – allocate a specific amount of time (perhaps over several lessons) and ask the students to work collaboratively to design and create a language game which will be used in class to test specific knowledge.

12 Fun with grammar – many students find grammar challenging to learn and apply correctly, so ask the students to design a short starter task in which they are expected to reteach an aspect of grammar to their peers in an innovative way.

13 Une minute/Trente secondes (see Chapter 3).

14 Neuf questions/Neun Fragen/Nueve preguntas (see Chapter 3).

15 Draw – students should draw a visual representation of aspects of the speaking task/dictation and label it as best they can. This should test their comprehension and understanding.

16 Random vocab surprise – ensure your learners are prepared for their terminal assessment (whether that is end-of-year/unit/key stage or GCSE/A level) by purposefully using unpopular and unfamiliar language to test their vocabulary knowledge. Alternatively, I give the students a word and ask them to come up with two or three synonyms.

17 Role play adventures – ask the students to create their own role plays in the international language to show you what they know. If you need to assess a specific range of tenses or vocabulary, share this with them so

they know it is an integral part of the task. Encourage them to be creative!

18 Quizzical questions – allocate specific questions to learners, ensuring that they demand an incremental level of detail on a specific topic or identified key language. Remind them not to repeat the exact same answers but to provide increasing levels of detail to demonstrate their language skills.

19 Translation tussle – select texts which the learners can access and translate, but make sure there are some red herrings, false friends or unfamiliar aspects with which they might struggle. The initial familiarity should enable them to read the text, but the tussle will come if there is more than one way to translate the language. To ensure success, model the process for the learners first, reminding them about how to approach and tussle with the language throughout the task. Give the students a generous amount of time for this task initially (depending on the level of challenge). They will speed up as they become more confident, so you can then start to reduce the time allocated.

20 Show me what you know – challenge your students to show you what they know through any medium they choose. Be clear on what you are testing or expecting to see, but give them free rein to be creative. Some students may need encouragement to be inventive if they are expecting a test. To be clear, I expect them to be creative not only in their use of language but also in how it is presented.

USING THE RIGHT LANGUAGE

Instead of using the term listening/speaking/reading/writing test, I use one of these alternative names; although the tasks are still assessments, the terminology causes less anxiety for learners. I don't want my students to be overwhelmed or distressed due to overthinking or negative thoughts about assessment, so I use other opportunities to track, monitor and assess their progress. By disguising the assessment, I often find both students and their parents enquiring about when the tests are to be administered; they are often surprised, and pleased, to learn they have already taken place! I'm all for preparing students for real-life assessments because these are unavoidable, but in the classroom we can seek to avoid the self-limiting and self-deprecating thoughts that can keep learners awake or cause symptoms of physical stress such as sickness, shaking and tears.

Students aren't daft; they know what a traditional test paper and test conditions look like. However, reframing the assessment as a 'show me what you know' task can diminish anxiety and enable all students to cultivate a positive mindset. If the same vocabulary that is used in the everyday classroom is applied to terminal assessments, including GCSE and A level exams, the stakes can be lowered. The students know they have completed activities like these many times before, so they are well-prepared psychologically.

Preparing learners for assessments doesn't have to be harsh, cold and fear inducing. We can extend humanity and kindness and create an environment in which students can flourish and respond to the challenge without fear and apprehension. It's all in the planning and mindset. Informing students about expectations and parameters is important, but so is exam technique if we want them to achieve their personal target or indeed beyond it. Even as terminal assessments become increasing rigorous and exam preparation and revision remain big business, I truly believe that this should not come at the expense of learning. The exclusion of certain elements of topics, or indeed whole subjects, from the curriculum in favour of exam techniques does not serve our learners well. Preparation is a part of the learning experience, but it should not dominate. Languages are about communication and making yourself understood to others; it should never be about learning huge sections of text by rote to regurgitate for a specific exam. That isn't language learning; it's an insult to the beauty of language.

At GCSE and A level, it is essential for students to be able to operate successfully in two languages, but it is also important for them to be able to decipher what the question is actually asking. (Is exam rubric a third language?) Unfortunately, language exams are not simply a test of knowledge and the ability to manipulate language to communicate successfully, or an opportunity to demonstrate skill, range and depth of understanding. There is also the added challenge of acquiring good exam technique so the students can access questions, understand what is being asked of them and hit on the one or two vocabulary items required for their answers to be accepted.

Unfortunately, 'accepted' and 'rejected' language crops up in both listening and reading exams, as well as for translation, which is very frustrating. Exam boards demand not only understanding and translation skills but also specific vocabulary. I teach students to show their understanding not through literal translation, but by using a range of language which hopefully infers the answer, if not using the exact word. In translation tasks this is absolutely correct: the translated text needs to read well in the target language. However, in listening and reading responses the students must supply a specific word, so the exam can become a guessing game rather than marks being awarded for a good answer. Check examiners' reports for more details of accepted and rejected language.

Mindset is vital for exam success, so we need to ensure that our students are 'match fit' for their language assessments. Months beforehand, I take the students through the exam process by walking them to the exam hall, sitting them down at the desks and getting them to complete a paper. We also spend some time in the space talking about what will happen on the day and how to organise their time, so there are no surprises and no missed questions. When students tell me they are going to fail, I remind them of the mindset practice we have done together to mentally prepare them for each of the four terminal assessments they have to complete and remind them to do their best with a smile.

I like to lead a final 'revision breakfast' on the day of the listening and reading exams, as these sit back to back and are a significant source of stress. I want to see the learners before the exam and encourage them to laugh and smile, eat some breakfast and get hydrated. We also do various activities to ease their worries, such as remembering top tips for the first five minutes of the exam and revisiting the exam rubric. This is a great opportunity to make sure the students are warmed up to the language, so we recall vocabulary and spend some time listening in the language on which they are going to be examined. I cannot emphasise enough the importance of this because listening is perceived to be the hardest language skill to master.

THE POWER OF LUCKY SOCKS

The breakfast session is a positive experience for all those who attend, not least because I bring out a final secret weapon: a pair of lucky socks! There is a brightly coloured pair for every member of the class. I inform them that in recent months the lucky socks have been 'blessed' by every deity known to man, as well as sprinkled with fairy, unicorn and pixie dust for extra luck. The students either love them, laugh or think I have finally lost the plot, but they are always accepted, and the students put them on with a grin. As the session ends, we walk together proudly – socks on, heads up, smiles broad and walking tall – through the throng of students towards the exam hall. The students are ready for anything. Onlookers tend to laugh or smile, but the crowds part and let us through; the staff know exactly what I am doing and why. It is all about having a positive mindset and boosting confidence. I want my learners to enter the exam hall believing they can answer every question and gain full marks. And if that takes a pair of multicoloured socks, then so be it.

By chance, I recently met a former student – now a successful adult with two scientific degrees to his name. He skipped towards me and animatedly shared updates of his own life and that of his lovely parents. I was impressed by his globe-trotting success. However, I was astounded when he told me that he still had the lucky socks I had given him when he was 15 years old, just before a GCSE speaking test, and that they had been on his feet for every exam he had taken ever since. And he had yet to wash the socks as he didn't want to 'wash the luck out of them'! I was both horrified, as it was almost 13 years since I had given him the socks, and secretly delighted that he still had them and that they still meant something to him. For this student, like many others, the socks were a talisman to bolster his confidence, and it had worked.

Some professional sports people have rituals which they perform systematically before a big event, including having lucky items which they must have about them or wear. If this type of positive thinking strategy works psychologically, and it isn't hurting anyone, then it is definitely worth trialling. Socks don't have to be expensive – it is a small gesture. They can be purchased in multipacks from all good supermarkets – the brighter and more colourful the better (don't forget to purchase a range of sizes). You do need to be confident, show a sense of humour and have a good relationship with your students, as well as being brave enough to wear a pair of the socks yourself – yes, even over the clothes you put on that morning! It's all part of the impact; it's definitely worth it when you see their anxiety fade and confidence grow. Preparing students for exams is important and having lucky socks, as daft as it may seem to some, might be just what your students need to help them believe in themselves that little bit more.

REVISION, LEARNING AND EXAM TECHNIQUE

Preparation for terminal assessments – whether they are end-of-year/key stage, GCSE or A level exams – should take place across the academic year while the learning is happening. The assessments may even drive the creation and structure of schemes of learning. The revision of vocabulary, grammar and key terminology should be interwoven into the teaching, with continued recall of previously learned language which is reinforced through frequent, spaced low-stakes testing. Gone are the days of starting revision once the course has been taught. (At least, I hope so.)

Schemes of learning should be structured using the programmes of study to ensure that learners are well-prepared for unit assessments and terminal exams. However, just to be clear, this is not about teaching to the test. Languages departments need to identify exactly what they want their students to learn and what skills they need to develop throughout the year, so they can successfully reach the ambitious outcomes identified for them – linguistically, grammatically and culturally. Constructing the curriculum around these aspirations, the learners and the key elements, as well as language and life skills, is vital to make sure that the right curriculum is developed for your students in your setting, which prepares them for languages success beyond school. This should be reflected in the mapping of skills, grammar and language across the units of learning, the year and the key stage, and not based on what you think is likely to appear in the exam.

This means that the curriculum is no longer structured around teaching to the test or the textbook – thankfully. Of course we need to assess our students, and they should be tracked and closely monitored to ensure they are making progress and reaching or surpassing their potential. Once the curriculum has been agreed, it is essential that there are opportunities for spaced practice. Key vocabulary, grammar and structures should be recalled throughout each topic, not simply ticked off at the end of the unit. Rehearsing previously learned language and grammatical structures improves memory and recall and reduces the amount of language that students forget. For example, we don't teach a tense and then use it only once within a topic or theme. Grammar, like much of the language, is reused and therefore it must be recalled and recycled across the course, year and key stage.

We need to ask our students what they know (perhaps call it a 'pre-test') and identify their prior learning *before* we commence teaching. Many schools use baseline assessments[1] as a starting point, so that at the end of the unit, series of teaching or academic year the students can complete a low-stakes test to indicate what they have learned. Some of the creative alternatives to assessment listed earlier in this chapter are fantastic to use here too. Following formative assessment and feedback, the students should revisit their work through DIRT, which will give them an opportunity to go through the activity/task/test to see if they can correct any errors or develop their work in response to the feedback.

Interestingly, asking students to identify what they know before starting a new topic will in itself result in learning, as it promotes the transference of language, grammatical structures and key phrases. It also reinforces language learning and encourages students to remember what they can do and when they last did it. Reminding students of past learning experiences, whether successful or challenging, is always beneficial. Their successes can be built on, enriched and extended, and previous difficulties can be analysed and overcome. Making learning experiences memorable helps because when memories are recalled, the more abstract memories are remembered first.

When asking learners to retrieve specific information, make sure that any misconceptions or errors that emerge

---

1 Baseline assessments score the performance of learners within a few weeks of them starting school in Reception or secondary (Year 7). The assessment focuses chiefly on the students' literacy and numeracy; however, they are increasingly being used to measure knowledge and skills across all subjects. Baseline assessment in MFL usually commences in secondary school.

are addressed and corrected to ensure the learning is secure. When a new language is learned mistakes inevitably occur, which is why timely marking, assessment and feedback are essential. The wonderful thing about learning a language is that vocabulary and grammar are transferable across a range of topics, so retrieval can be built on as each new topic is introduced. When given the opportunity our students can embellish the language we have given them to produce creative, engaging and personal output. Through opportunities to retrieve and recall, recycle and elaborate in well-planned tasks and challenges – such as best sentence/paragraph, short story, opinion piece or poem – we see not only developments in their language skills but also increased confidence, range and fluency.

Interleaving and interweaving language throughout the unit of study helps to promote an increased awareness of the structure of language and how it works (so we alternate (interleave) back and forth between topics and ensure that key components, such as grammar, are interwoven throughout the course of study). This type of sequenced learning has been shown to benefit both recall and transferability.[2] Create opportunities for the students to show you what they know via a range of tasks which develop all four language skills as well as translation. This will provide evidence of the learners' knowledge, understanding and skills, while also providing robust information to report back to parents and the SLT. Timely feedback which recognises students' efforts and achievements against the criteria, as well as pointers during DIRT, enables learners to collate a series of self-created model answers, whether they are spoken, written or translated

---

2   For a brief review, see H. Webb, Revision Techniques: Interleaving and Spacing, *SecEd* (3 April 2019). Available at: http://www.sec-ed.co.uk/best-practice/revision-techniques-interleaving-and-spacing/.

pieces. These can form a portfolio of success which should be celebrated and stored for when students need to be reminded of what they are capable of and what they can achieve.

School systems require that formal assessments take place, although an increasing number of schools are moving to end-of-year assessments in addition to the end-of-unit assessments that some MFL departments carry out to ensure that up-to-date data is available. These assessments should be closely aligned with the curriculum in order to accurately measure learning and progress, rather than testing learners for the sake of it. As we have seen in this chapter, there are more creative ways to measure learning and ensure the students have absorbed, understood and can apply what they have been taught than by completing a range of endless tests.

THIRTY REVISION STRATEGIES FOR THE MFL CLASSROOM

If students are well-practised in retrieving language and recycling it with increasing confidence in the four areas of language skill – listening, speaking, reading and writing – then revision just means more of this.

1. MFL PREPARATION PLAN

Students need support and structure, and this logical step-by-step guide is designed to provide that outside of school. It provides clear guidance, which allows the student (parent, carer or tutor) to work through the eight elements of revision.

GCSE PERSONAL PREPARATION GAME PLAN[3]

1. Goal is in focus	1.1	You have a clear goal of exam success.	
	1.2	You are willing to receive advice.	
	1.3	You are in a position to act on advice.	
	1.4	You know where to seek advice.	
2. Revision context	2.1	You are able to devote sufficient time to revision.	
	2.2	You have a suitable place in which to revise.	
	2.3	You have committed to a revision programme.	
	2.4	You have the subject materials you need to revise from and use them.	
	2.5	You have the resource materials to construct revision notes from.	
3. Revision programme	3.1	You know the dates of your exams.	
	3.2	You know how many papers you need to sit and what each one is on.	
	3.3	You know the kinds of things you may be asked to do on each paper.	

---

3 Thanks to Andy Philip Day who kindly shared this strategy with me. (Note the code used here: L = listening, S = speaking, W = writing, R = reading.)

	3.4	You know what skills you may be required to show.	
	3.5	You have drawn up a revision timetable.	
	3.6	You are aware of the importance of interleaving your revision.	
4. Revision process	4.1	You are aware of different revision techniques.	
	4.2	You have selected the techniques that work best for you.	
	4.3	You self-check to ensure your revision techniques are effective.	
5. Applying the revision	5.1	You know which tier of exam you have been entered for (higher or foundation).	
	5.2	You know where to find past papers and Edexcel examWizard papers.	
	5.3	You have attempted past papers and Edexcel examWizard papers.	
	5.4	You know where to find mark schemes.	
	5.5	You have used mark schemes to check your practice answers.	
6. Tackling exam questions	6.1	You read the questions carefully and know how many there are to complete.	
	6.2	You interpret questions accurately – you get what they are about (e.g. topic, tense).	

6.3	You know who the sub-question(s) is (are) about.	
6.4	You make notes during the reading time to pre-empt possible answers. (L)	
6.5	You listen to the instructions and the example and use the time to reread the questions.	
6.6	You make the right number of points to be awarded all the marks available.	
6.7	You give clear and detailed answers, not generalised non-specific ones. (L, W)	
6.8	You make rich, detailed points which show that you think beyond the 'obvious'.	
6.9	You refer to the text, highlighting your answers to support checking. (R, W)	
6.10	You are aware of false friends, red herrings and other linguistic pitfalls. (L, R, W)	
6.11	You listen to each answer very carefully. (L)	
6.12	You don't miss questions out – either accidentally or by choice.	
6.13	You use the time effectively so all questions are given appropriate attention.	

	6.14	You answer the question in the correct language. (L, S, R, W)	
7. Writing to get your ideas across effectively	7.1	You write your answer using the lines/space effectively.	
	7.2	Your writing is legible and easy to read.	
	7.3	You use full sentences (unless one-word/one-phrase answers are OK).	
	7.4	You use capital letters and full stops correctly.	
	7.5	You identify and recheck answers to the spelling, punctuation and grammar (SPaG) questions.	
	7.6	You correct common errors (e.g. verb formation and endings, subject pronouns, spellings, agreement, negatives, word order).	
	7.7	You use vocabulary and tenses accurately.	
	7.8	You complete longer answers which offer more marks carefully.	
	7.9	You sustain focus throughout the paper – the last answers are as good as the first ones.	
8. Well-being	8.1	You are getting sufficient sleep.	
	8.2	You are getting the right kind of nutrition.	
	8.3	You are able to handle the stress.	

8.4	You have an effective support/help network when it is needed.	
8.5	You are able to derive satisfaction from the process of exam preparation.	
8.6	You know when you need help and ask for it from peers, parents and teachers.	

When emailed out as a 'how to help' document, parents find it extremely useful, as it provides prompts and conversation starters to help students with MFL revision. It can be placed at the front of revision folders or stuck on a fridge or pinboard. This template can be used at any level to give learners the support they need to help them revise effectively.

2. NEUF QUESTIONS/NEUN FRAGEN/ NUEVE PREGUNTAS

Nine questions has just as much impact as a revision tool as it does in the classroom (see Chapter 3). On an A4 grid, set out nine questions on a topic, theme or tense, as in the example on page 143. You could project this onto an interactive whiteboard or hand out printed sheets. Direct the students (individually or in groups) to read through these questions and think about their responses carefully before preparing an answer on paper or a sticky note. Nine questions can be a writing or speaking task.

1 Où vas-tu en vacances?	2 Tu préfères aller en vacances ou rester à la maison?	3 Tu es resté(e) combien de temps?
4 Qu'est-ce que tu as fait pendant tes vacances?	5 Qu'est-ce que tu as mangé?	6 Et le temps, il faisait comment?
7 Tu préfères aller en vacances avec ta famille ou tes amis?	8 Où iras-tu l'année prochaine pour tes vacances?	9 Voudrais-tu y retourner en vacances?

3. RALLY ROBIN RECALL

This activity allows students to retrieve and recall key language and grammatical structures, warming up their brains. As they move through each level the language challenge increases, which students find less threatening than advancing immediately to level 3. The levels also allow them to recycle the language their peers may have given them during the process.

Level 1: Set a topic or question to pairs or groups. The students should list all the items of vocabulary and phrases they can, taking it in turns to do so. They must not repeat previously mentioned vocabulary, chunks or phrases.

Level 2: Pose a question and give the students some thinking time. They should then share aloud topic vocabulary and interesting or complex structures from which to build sentences or grammatical structures using CORTED or TAILORED (see Chapter 3). Sharing with one another in this way reminds students of some of the vocabulary, grammatical structures, connectives, comparatives or superlative phrases that they could use.

Level 3: Following on from level 2, the students can start to build sentences, taking it in turns to develop interesting longer sentences and responses, adding to their own or their peers' responses or challenging a response already given. The students should construct answers of between 30 seconds and one minute in length using CORTED or TAILORED.

4. MNEMONICS CHECK

Ask the students to use the mnemonics CORTED or TAILORED to ensure they are producing interesting written work and spoken responses using all of the different elements. You could also encourage students to develop a deeper understanding of a text by using these mnemonics to deconstruct a particular passage.

5. A–Z

The students should use the 26 letters of the alphabet to identify phrases and individual pieces or chunks of vocabulary, or to create sentences across specific topics. 'A–Z' can also be used to revise grammar and tenses. This recall activity can prove very challenging for some letters, but is good revision practice.

6. REVISION T-SHIRTS

Issue each student with a T-shirt and some permanent markers or fabric pens so they can populate it with the vocabulary they struggle to remember. (Other schools have used this technique to create revision scarves.) The point is that the students focus individually on what they need to recall, and do so in a visual, creative and relaxed way.

7. TOP 100 WORDS

Using recent examiners' reports, create one list of the 100 most popular words and phrases for students to learn, and a second list containing the vocabulary that the candidates did not know. Rather than supplying the vocabulary as a list, present it as a word cloud so the students have to seek out the information themselves (I like http://www.wordclouds.com). Encourage them to learn these words using a look, cover, write, check strategy (see strategy 21 on page 151).

8. COLLECT RANDOM VOCAB

Terminal exams are full of interesting words and unfamiliar phrases, so ask the students to keep a record of peculiar language they have come across and learn these terms. These could be synonyms. Vocabulary and phrase snap is a fun vocabulary revision game for pairs of students.

9. PAPER CHAIN COMPLEXITY

The students are expected to build brilliant sentences and texts by breaking down their written pieces and transferring the different elements onto paper strips in order to build up sentences. The chains can be also adjusted or extended to develop original new sentences. This strategy helps students to remember chunks of complex phrasing.

10. CHANNEL YOUR INNER JACK

Many comedians, celebrities and politicians punctuate their performances, speeches and interviews with short punchy phrases. These are their 'go-to elements', which embellish the point being made and give it additional meaning. Encourage students to select ten fantastic phrases or chunks of interesting language to add to their pieces and to channel their inner Jack (or role model). For example, we don't tend to use 'après avoir'/'après être' phrases daily, but they can add a level of complexity to speech and writing. The students can sprinkle these staples throughout their work to create funny and interesting spoken and written pieces. This strategy tends to result in more impressive pieces of work, which are more easily produced because the students can recycle these elements. This superb strategy aids speaking and writing revision through recall and repeat practice.

11. SHOW ME WHAT YOU KNOW

Select a topic and ask the students to write down everything they know about it. It could be random words, a piece of poetry, a cartoon, a short story, a knowledge poster, a mind map – let the students decide. They should complete these tasks across a range of topics to ensure that they revise all the themes and related topics within the GCSE syllabus.

12. BEST 30/50/100/150 WORDS

Encourage the students to practise writing excellent-quality 30-, 50-, 100- and 150-word written pieces on a variety of topics. They should check that the key elements and phrases are present and that they are using a range of tenses. They can use sticky notes to devise a plan of action, bullet pointing the areas they want to cover so that nothing is forgotten.

13. PAST PAPER FUN

Completing past papers is a great way to brush up on exam techniques and strategies. Don't time the papers initially, just ask the students to work through them. You can introduce timed responses as their confidence improves. Get the students to mark each other's papers and give feedback on how well they have completed them. This works brilliantly as a motivational tool and provides insight into how to avoid daft errors when sitting exams.

14. BE SPECIFIC (MARK SCHEME FUN)

Give the students mark schemes to check their answers in listening, reading and writing (translation only) questions to ensure they meet the necessary criteria. In this way, the students will learn to improve their responses using precise, signposted language and to improve their exam technique.

15. LISTENING PRACTICE

Encourage the students to listen frequently to authentic language videos and audio to improve their understanding and skills in preparation for the listening assessment. They could access This is Language (www.thisislanguage.com), YouTube videos, podcasts or news channel sites for variety. You could also recycle the bank of listening videos you have created and collated for this purpose.

16. LISTENING 3-2-1

When the students are listening to a film, video or recording, ask them to note down key language using 3-2-1 from CORTED or TAILORED (see Chapter 3). It's up to you as the teacher to decide what you want the students to find: it could be three opinions or three points; two reasons providing justification for the opinions identified or two time-frames/time-specific phrases; and one complex phrase or one unknown word. This strategy should reinforce the key language you need them to know but it should also serve as good repeat practice for listening.

17. RANDOM VOCAB SURPRISE

In groups, ask the students to identify ten words, phrases or chunks from a range of topics and create a translation test. Five could be in English and five in the international language, or they could all be in the international language, and the more peculiar the better. Encourage students to go for synonyms, and not for the obvious, to add challenge.

18. DICTATION

For this task, the students should create a short spoken piece (perhaps two or three sentences) which can be used as a dictation and shared with a friend for them to write out. The students can then swap roles. The more creative the writing, the better the task. Alternatively, if you have used an interesting text in the classroom, select a few sentences from it and use these for dictation. Dictation is great for revision as it helps the students to practise listening to long strings of words on the lookout for specific information. It also improves their vocabulary and grammar.

19. REVISION CUE CARDS/DRAW CARDS/TRANSLATE CARDS

Get the students to create some revision cue cards by writing relevant vocabulary and grammar on an old set of playing cards. They should select one card and then revise the language, complete translations and find listening exercises or recordings to immerse themselves in the topic language.

You can also ask them to create knowledge posters or minds maps to recall the language they know. Alternatively, they can show you exactly what they know by recording a short spoken piece or by writing a 30/50/100/150-word piece in preparation for exam questions which will ask for answers of this length. Encourage the learners to add to these revision aids over time, or even to swap with their peers and add to one another's work. This encourages learners to collaborate with one another and to review and extend their own work.

Draw cards are created in a similar way to cue cards and can be prepared for any difficult-to-remember topics. The students should draw a picture relating to a topic (e.g. holidays) on a sheet of blank card and then label it (alternatively, they can find an image instead). They should then create a short written or spoken piece using the vocabulary. They can revise the topic using tenses and opinions: past holiday, ideal holiday, usual holiday arrangements, disastrous holiday, future holiday, best/worst holiday and so on. This visual task draws on students' experience of dual coding and aids with the recall of vocabulary and grammar. It also helps to promote the transferability of language structures and can serve as a prompt when developing longer written or spoken pieces.

Translation cards (cards created by the teacher containing text for the students to translate) draw on the speaking work the students will have done throughout their course. If a translation booklet has been issued, direct the learners to use this to practise translating from and into the target language. Alternatively, you could create a series of subject-specific translation pocket cards for your class. I always have a bank of real texts from news stories and literature on hand for added variety (which also double up as dictation tasks). Equally, if the students have produced some fantastic work, why not use this for translation? The individuals love it, and it results in less work for you as a busy teacher.

20. GAMIFY IT

Creating a game is a great way for students to revise key language. A board game could revise numbers, prices, weather or times. Encourage the students to play the game with friends and revise together. Alternatively, get your tech-savvy learners to develop an app.

21. LOOK, COVER, WRITE, CHECK

Look, cover, write, check is fantastic way for learners to practise phonics, vocabulary and phrases independently. An often-forgotten, simple strategy, it can be easily taught and used in the languages classroom – especially for revision – to recall and reinforce key language, grammar and terminology.

22. THIRTY CIRCLES[4]

Using a thirty circles sheet, the students should select a topic from a cue card or a theme and fill in the thirty circles with language from the topic. These could be individual words, chunks, phrases, complete sentences, a story or a poem. They should keep going until they have filled in every circle. This aids revision through retrieval and recall, but it is more fun than simply writing words in their exercise books or on scrap paper. The students can also dual code their thirty circles sheets – they are very versatile!

23. QUIZ TIME

Ask the students to create mini tests and quizzes for themselves and for friends. They can swap these and test one another. Make sure they check the answers carefully.

---

4 Tom Kelley and David Kelley have created a brilliant resource. Resource: 30 Circles – Creativity Challenge, *UKEdChat* (27 May 2014). Available at: https://ukedchat.com/2014/05/27/resource-30-circles-creativity-challenge.

24. TRANSLATION TIME

Either using resources provided by you or an extract from a news website, the students should select eight lines of text and translate them. This task can be done individually or in pairs.

25. FUN WITH GRAMMAR

It is important that students revise grammar in order to develop their range and confidence in using it. The 'A–Z' or 'Thirty circles' strategies can be used to generate grammatical phrases to boost spoken and written work. Grammar games, played individually or with others, also help students to conjugate verbs and recognise endings and structures. Learners love to create their own games, quizzes and activities to test their own and their peers' grammatical knowledge and skills.

26. Q&A

In pairs, ask the students to take it in turns asking questions from a speaking booklet and generating answers after a set period of thinking time. They should simply read aloud what they have prepared previously. This is like 'Rally Robin recall' but with questions.

27. ROLE PLAY REVISION

Select a role play topic and ask the students to practise with a friend/parent/older sibling. They should take on different roles and try to identify and note down any common themes that might help them with the types of questions they are likely to face in the speaking exam.

28. PICTURE CARD MOMENTS

Ask the students to select a topic, choose an image from the internet and create a 45-second spoken piece on what they can see (you can adjust the time depending on the learners' language levels). Learners should complete these frequently across the GCSE themes and a range of topics to practise and revise the language.

29. UNE MINUTE, S'IL VOUS PLAÎT/ EINE MINUTE, BITTE/UN MINUTO, POR FAVOR

As well as a great classroom activity, this is also an excellent revision strategy. As the students are so used to doing this in class, they can revise well for a speaking assessment using the same technique. Select a topic and ask the students to generate an oral presentation lasting one minute in the target language. This is best used after 'Nine questions' or 'A–Z'. This is a spoken piece, not a reading revision task, so the learners should not read from prepared notes (other than brief bullet points).

30. PLAN YOUR REVISION

Get the students to create a revision timetable for all four aspects of the MFL exams: listening, speaking, reading and writing. They are all equally weighted and therefore demand equal revision time if the students are to be successful. The speaking exam always comes first at GCSE and A level, so the students should prioritise this, but not at the expense of the other skills. They should avoid leaving any of their revision until the last minute.

Students should aim to revise in short bursts of no longer than 45 minutes in each sitting. Remind them of the spaced retrieval practice they have completed throughout the course. Encourage them to evidence their revision to guard against simply 'reading through'; numerous research studies have shown that this is not an effective revision strategy.

FIFTEEN STRATEGIES TO IMPROVE EXAM TECHNIQUE

One area that has perhaps been slightly overlooked within MFL is teaching students about exam technique – helping them to understand what the questions are actually asking and homing in on the specific language that exam boards require. Here are some tips you can pass on to your students.

1   Use exam time productively. Know what to do in the first five minutes of each exam: stay calm by focusing on your breathing, check you have the correct exam paper (especially if tiers are involved), read the exam paper from front to back and highlight the key information that is required (see below).

2   Highlight the marks available on every page and every question for the listening, reading and writing papers.

3   Highlight the rubric, especially in which language the question should be answered.

4   How many questions across how many pages? Identify how many parts there are to each question and across how many pages.

5 Write a line, miss a line. It is always better to write on alternate lines to give yourself space to add, correct or change language and ensure that it remains clear.

6 Read the questions to contextualise the text. In the reading exam, identify what you are being asked to answer before reading the dense text.

7 Highlight your answers. Highlight or underline the answers you find in a text. It will help you to check they are correct later. Number or letter these if this is helpful.

8 Ch-ch-check it out. Does your translation read correctly? Does it sound weird or clunky? Make sure it reads like something someone would say.

9 Count your answers, leaving no gaps, blanks or unanswered questions. You highlighted the number of marks at the start of the exam, so check that you have given enough detail to gain full marks.

10 Educated guess. Don't ever miss out a question; make an educated guess based on the context. You might gain a mark or even get it right. A blank is always wrong.

11 You have five minutes of reading time in the listening test. Use this time efficiently and effectively, as you have practised.

12 Use the long pauses before each question in the listening test to reread the questions and all of the potential answers.

13 TAILORED speaking and writing. Check that your work contains the key elements you have revised to communicate your message.

14 Look out for signposts. In the reading and listening papers signposts will be indicated through tenses; depending on the level there may be a range of tenses. Make sure you know how to find and understand the signposts and additional information to complete the questions correctly.

15 On completion of the last question, read through each question and the rest of the paper in reverse, checking you have answered every question as best and as fully as you can.

CHAPTER 8

HOW TO MAKE BEST USE OF YOUR FOREIGN LANGUAGE ASSISTANT AND TEACHING ASSISTANT

FOREIGN LANGUAGE ASSISTANTS

Allowing your FLA or exchange teacher to contribute fully to your department requires careful consideration, not least because we have another human being with a wealth of experiences and expertise to share, which is a cause for celebration. Enabling your FLA/exchange teacher to contribute to maximum effect may require facilitation, guidance or at least a discussion in which you share your expectations. In this way, we are empowering the new member of our team to get involved in a professional capacity, which can only add value and enrich the language learning experience for the learners.

- Treating and valuing your FLA/exchange teacher as another member of the languages team, and supporting them as you would a new teacher, is always a good start. Go through key documentation, school policies, conduct and safeguarding and give them a pass, keys, ICT account, staff badge, school handbook, diary/planner and access to all MFL rooms. They need to be clear on your expectations but also feel part of the team, as well as having access to everything they need.

- Allow your FLA/exchange teacher's individual personality to come alive by encouraging them to share their experiences, home life, culture and traditions; it will be eye-opening and inspiring for the learners. You should also enable them to be themselves professionally. This will deepen the students' knowledge of other cultures as well as promote tolerance in line with the school's work on British values.

- Set up a timetable with a range of classes and teachers across the department, but make sure you are available to give support as necessary. I used to meet FLAs and exchange teachers fortnightly, the same as I would for teachers in the team, so make time for this too.

- Ensure that the FLA/exchange teacher has a space where they can work. Book this if necessary to ensure that it is not taken by other staff.

- Focus on speaking. Native speakers can be wonderful in developing learners' oral confidence and skill through small group work. These out-of-class experiences provide a real opportunity for peer-to-peer speaking in the international language, which always needs lots of encouragement. Group learners carefully to ensure they all participate and have a positive experience. Support your FLA/

exchange teacher by checking in with them after the sessions.

- Close the feedback loop. Working in small groups allows the FLA/exchange teacher to really focus on helping students to address any misconceptions or issues that have arisen in the classroom.

- Don't forget culture. We can't all be experts in all languages all of the time. Encourage your FLA/ exchange teacher to contribute by updating tired or overused websites, bringing in fresh resources, music, magazines, ideas, games, activities, reading materials and so on. FLAs are a wealth of information, but give them time to settle and get to know your schemes of learning/work so they can make suggestions.

- Assemblies. Exchange teachers and FLAs have so much to share, so it is fantastic if you can encourage and support them to lead an assembly. It can be memorable for all parties if they can make contact with all the year groups in the school.

- Native speaker videos. Once furnished with a digital device – be it a school iPad or tablet – videos on specific vocabulary, topics or grammar can be created which will help to develop learners' listening skills through exposure to another voice. These can be used for years to come.

- Urge your FLA/exchange teacher to add to the enrichment of MFL by leading on activities such as inter-year-group or school language competitions (local and national), creative projects, debate and discussion clubs, film clubs and so on.

- Your FLA/exchange teacher might be able to suggest additional reading or literary texts that will enrich or extend what your department currently has in place.

These are just a few ideas to ensure that we welcome our FLAs and exchange teachers into the team. I'm sure you will have thought of many more to maximise and learn from them, so the department, resources and, of course, the individuals themselves become much richer from their time with us.

TEACHING ASSISTANTS

Like FLAs, teaching assistants are worth their weight in gold. MFL teachers should always appreciate having TAs in the classroom because they have so many wonderful qualities, skills and talents. The TA's primary role is to support the learners, but this can also include learning a foreign language themselves, not only to motivate learners but also to support their engagement and progress. In my experience, the added element of competition has been a superb incentive for some learners – the chance to beat your TA is an opportunity too good to be missed!

However, it is a sad fact that TAs are disappearing from MFL classrooms to fulfil other needs that are perceived to be more important. In some schools, all students with special educational needs and disabilities (SEND) or additional learning needs (ALN)[1] have been withdrawn from MFL. This is a tragedy for these young people and represents the failure to deliver a fair and inclusive education system.

- Welcome working with your TA – you will soon grow to love them.

- Make sure your TA knows what effective support looks like in the MFL classroom. This means meeting with

---

1   ALN is used widely in Wales, and increasingly beyond, as the preferred acronym.

them prior to lessons. This doesn't have to be every lesson, but perhaps every two weeks with email updates in-between. TAs are busy people too.

- Share schemes of learning and lesson plans so that TAs can get an overview of the series of lessons over time. This will help them to plan effective support. Allocate a space in the departmental office so they have somewhere to work and give them access to the resources they need. On some occasions, I have given my TAs exercise books so they can make their own notes and develop their own language skills.

- If your TA isn't confident with languages, ask them what you can do to support them. Don't let this be a barrier to them working effectively in the department.

- Bounce ideas off your TA. Asking your TA for their thoughts and suggestions values their knowledge and expertise, and ultimately empowers them.

- Empower your TA to reward and praise learners in your classroom, and to discipline if need be. They are part of the school community so they should know the behaviour policy. Some TAs want to assist in this way but not all do, so be prepared for this and don't demand it.

- Your TA is likely to know the students better than you do; it is possible that they support some individuals across several subjects. Pick their brains because they may have an insight into how to engage and inspire the learners. Encourage them to share this information with you to help create a great MFL learning experience.

- Remember that your TA is there to help the learners, not to do the photocopying. Respect them and appreciate their role.

- If you want your TA to improve learners' independence and engagement, or to devise more structured interventions, then agree this with them in advance. You will also need to share what this will look like in MFL and be sure they are confident in achieving this. Some TAs may require extra support.

- Make sure that you communicate frequently with your TA so they can provide feedback on interventions and student progress. This could be through email or a more formal meeting.

- Invite your TA to your departmental meetings so they feel involved. They may have other commitments elsewhere, but always extend the invitation so they have the opportunity to contribute. If your TA does attend, make sure the agenda is ordered appropriately so they are not sitting through lots of irrelevant items.

- Decide and manage together with your TA what is best for your SEND/ALN learners – for example, support within the whole class or smaller group work in another space. Be aware that when students are out of the classroom they are missing out on your expertise.

- When trialling a new strategy, speak to your TA to ensure that the learners they support have the scaffolding they need to access the learning and make progress, but also to make sure that it will not cause upset or anxiety.

- If your TA is a more confident linguist, or one who is prepared to have a go, ask them to help prepare short videos, model tasks and expectations, remind learners of outcomes and take part in enrichment days and activities.

- When co-constructing with learners or reviewing lessons, units of learning or the scheme of learning, ask your TA for their opinions and contributions. It is worthwhile remembering that TAs go into many lessons so they may have a valuable broader perspective.

- Appreciate and look after your TA as you would any teacher in your team; in turn, they will look after you.

TAs can be lots of fun in lessons, not least because they are active learners who, in addition to supporting youngsters and the teacher, are also improving their own language skills. I have always enjoyed having TAs in my classroom, some of whom (like the learners) have not always had a positive prior experience with MFL, but who have enjoyed the lessons and genuinely felt like part of the class and the department. Good relationships are vital; if these are based on mutual respect, unconditional positive regard, professionalism and effective communication, then it will be an enriching experience for all.

I have known wonderful TAs who have gone on to become fantastic classroom practitioners in a range of subjects, including MFL. Some held back because of a lack of confidence, despite having a languages degree, but the experience of being in an MFL classroom pushed them to do it. Unless you get to know your TAs, you will never know what amazing skills, attributes and ideas they may have.

STUDENTS WITH SEND AND ALN IN THE MFL CLASSROOM

Every young person has the right to learn an international language, and it is our job as MFL practitioners to ensure that all learners can fully access the international language being taught. We do this by planning appropriately and providing support that is tailored to the needs of the learner. This enables them to build their knowledge, language skills and cultural understanding, like every other learner who enters our learning space. We want them to access the language fully, to enjoy it, to learn and to make great progress.

It starts with knowing your learners really well. You may have been given information about a student's educational needs and abilities, and perhaps also an education, health and care plan (EHCP), by your school's SEND/ALN coordinator, but it is always best to meet the young learner in person. This may entail visiting their current school, where you can introduce yourself and find out a little more about them. If necessary, Skype or FaceTime can also work well. I think that any good professional relationship benefits from spending time getting to know the learner, their likes and dislikes, and their language experience to date. In the case of learners with SEND/ALN, this will require precious time and organisation, but it can prove invaluable in understanding a vulnerable student's needs and preferences. For instance, for an individual who needs assistance travelling to and entering the classroom, arriving to face a class who are already seated, and in front of an unknown adult, does not make for a great beginning.

I have been fortunate enough to have worked with some fantastic TAs who have really helped me and my colleagues when meeting students with SEND/ALN face-to-face for the first time. Getting to know learners can go some way to easing anxieties and concerns for teacher and student, and parents/carers. Simply communicating with one another lessens the tension, whether this is in person or through an interpreter or digital device (if the individual has communication difficulties). If the student needs extra support, make sure the TA attends the meeting too, so the new school experience starts seamlessly. Aim to set up an initial meeting when the young person joins the school or prior to the first lesson with a new teacher. Subsequently, the learner might be invited to visit the learning space so they can assess how far they have to travel and the layout of the room. It could be that they request to sit in a specific place, for example, so this meeting gives them an opportunity to choose a suitable spot.

During the meeting I would provide an exercise book or digital device containing an overview of the learning for the year. It is important for young people to know what they will be learning, regardless of age, stage or ability, so take the time to go through this with them. Any learner coming into my classroom knows that I have the highest expectations for and of them, that I will meet them and their needs halfway, and that no question is ever a daft question.

I may show them work from other learners' books so they can get a sense of the languages work they will be doing. I will also give them a list of additional materials they might need to access at home/out of school to support and reinforce their learning. I'm a great believer in experiential learning so my learning space is full of helpful, colourful displays that aid learning and celebrate learners' success. If appropriate, I might show the learner some of these too; I don't want to overwhelm them, only seek to welcome them. If the young person has specific questions they would like to ask, hopefully either I or their TA can answer them. TAs are often brilliant in making sure that the conversation remains upbeat and positive. In this way, the learners know who their teacher is and where they will sit, they have a plan and they have access to resources to support them, all of which helps to ease any nervousness.

Increasingly, there are more learners with SEND/ALN in our classrooms, but if we know the students well and take time to find out about them and their requirements, we can fully support them with excellent learning experiences which are differentiated and tailored to their individual needs, as per the SEND code of practice.[2]

All educational establishments must make sure that special educational provision is high-quality, broad and balanced. Many schools, both mainstream and special, provide very successful language experiences, all of which are designed with the students' individual needs in mind. Sensory language experiences using music and song ensure that learners are exposed to various languages and dialects, while virtual tours, immersion rooms and green-screen technology promote rich language use and cultural diversity by taking learners to far-off lands which they may not be able to visit themselves. All of this provides a relevant and appropriate languages experience.

I find it immensely frustrating, therefore, that learners with SEND/ALN, who have an EHCP or qualify for pupil premium funding, are often withdrawn from MFL lessons because learning a language is perceived to be too hard for them, or because they need to focus on literacy in their first language or on another subject in which they are struggling. I would say, let's give the individual a chance

---

2 Department for Education and Department of Health and Social Care, *Special Educational Needs and Disability Code of Practice: 0 to 25 Years* (January 2015). Ref: DFE-00205-2013. Available at: https://www.gov.uk/government/publications/send-code-of-practice-0-to-25.

first and see how they get on. When reasonable adjustments are made, when clear and robust routines are in place, and when young people feel safe and secure, they often find that they enjoy learning another language and make progress.

Inclusion is not about segregation if the subject is challenging. The primary aim of inclusion is to provide *all* learners with access to a wide-ranging curriculum so they can develop communication and language skills, as well as confidence, knowledge, understanding and cultural capital alongside their peers. Inclusion also means that teachers must support their learners and plan appropriate languages experiences for the young people in front of them (we already do this so it's nothing new). When learners are withdrawn for half or even all of their international languages lessons and then sent back again (without the teacher being informed), it can be very challenging to ensure that learners feel successful when there are gaps in their knowledge due to absence, often through no fault of their own.

Languages teachers can, with time and prior notice, make sure learners feel welcomed, supported and included. Senior leaders and SEND/ALN coordinators need to communicate directly with languages teachers to ensure that they are fully informed of individual student's timetable alterations. I understand that difficult decisions have to be made, but it does appear that some learners are being denied the experience of learning another language and are therefore missing out on accessing a full curriculum.

To deliver a successful languages experience it is paramount to know the student. This gives me, as the teacher, the knowledge and understanding to best support the young person. Here are some considerations that you should always have at the forefront of your mind:

- What do I need to do to best support this learner to fully access the learning?

- What do they require to fully access the learning?

- What do I need to consider to ensure this learner can access the listening/speaking/reading/writing task that is specific to their learning needs?

- What does the learner need to fully access the listening/speaking/reading/writing task?
  - ▲ Dual-coded task.
  - ▲ Enlarged font.
  - ▲ Earphones.
  - ▲ Digital device.
  - ▲ Conversation strips.
  - ▲ Sentence builder jigsaws.

- What does the TA need to know about the listening/speaking/reading/writing task to best support the learner?

- What additional support does the learner need to feel success in the lesson today, or series of lessons?

- How will I use the TA in this lesson, or series of lessons, to ensure the learner feels success?

- What do I need to consider in the learning environment to best support the learner?
  - ▲ Noise levels.
  - ▲ Voice levels.
  - ▲ Grouping.
  - ▲ Space.

- ▲ Placement.

- ▲ Digital device.

- ▲ Earphones.

- ▲ Microphones.

- ▲ Realia.[3]

- ▲ Writing/whiteboard pen.

- ● Which scaffolding mat is required, and is this support appropriate for the learner?

  - ▲ Speaking.

  - ▲ Writing.

  - ▲ Sentence builder.

  - ▲ Grammar.

  - ▲ CORTED/TAILORED (see Chapter 3).

- ● Did anything arise in the last lesson that I need to be mindful of?

  - ▲ Build on professional relationship positively.

  - ▲ Provide resources as the learner was not in the lesson.

  - ▲ Evidence that the learner is making progress (over time).

- ● Do I have to discuss something specific with the learner?

  - ▲ Does the learner know how to make progress in MFL?

  - ▲ Does the learner know what progress looks like in MFL?

  - ▲ Does the learner have the appropriate support in language lessons?

---

3   Realia is the term used for real items that teachers collect and incorporate into their classroom practice.

- ▲ Feedback from a previous lesson.
- ▲ Information about a forthcoming lesson.
- ▲ Assessment.
- ● Do I have to discuss something specific with the TA?
  - ▲ Feedback from a previous lesson.
  - ▲ Information about a forthcoming lesson.
  - ▲ Assessment.
  - ▲ Revision.
  - ▲ Lesson tasks/planning.
  - ▲ How can progress be evidenced for the learner?
  - ▲ Is the learner making great progress? If not, what needs to be done about it? And who is responsible for this?

Many learners with SEND/ALN enjoy language lessons and achieve success. I have taught many students who, despite not enjoying some aspects of school and struggling in other subjects, have made fantastic progress when learning an international language, simply because it is something different. There have been several learners who struggled with dysgraphia; however, because adjustments were made (such as more appropriate exercise books) and digital devices were made available, these learners thrived and flourished in languages lessons. Because we knew these students and their significant adults, we communicated to ensure that the climate was right for the young person to be successful.

Interestingly, another learner had significant issues with handwriting when beginning at secondary school. He would write across four or five lines seemingly quite aggressively. But with time, patience, an appropriate exercise book, support and regular discussion with the TA, this decreased dramatically. The student's French book showed the best handwriting he had ever produced, closely followed by that in his Spanish book. In other lessons, this young person had refused to engage with writing tasks. As MFL teachers, we aimed to make sure that the classroom climate was primed to allow the students to thrive, and he rose to the challenge and set an example for other learners in the room.

I have also taught learners with selective mutism, who refused to speak in 95% of their lessons. Yet in languages they spoke an international language beautifully, albeit quietly (which frequently made me weep with joy on my drive home). I truly believe that if we pave the way for success for learners with SEND/ALN – through careful consideration, communicating and connecting with the student, striving to create the right climate for learning, and providing appropriate scaffolding and timely support – then they can learn an international language and make good progress.

There are ways and means to support all learners. Sometimes we have to turn to edtech and digital devices, seeking out video and recording apps to help reticent speakers or locating book creating apps to aid anxious writers or those with dexterity or mobility difficulties. We can devise games and projects; carefully craft conversation strips and sentence builder jigsaws; and scour scrapstores,[4] toyshops and charity shops and raid pound-shop shelves and bargain basements for objects we can use in the classroom. We can pack bags with food-based realia; set up a grocery store in our classroom; film cafés and restaurants; seek out online cookery videos; devise recipes and menus; and explore gastronomic experiences. We do all this to ensure that every learner can access language

---

4   Scrapstores (often charity or community interest groups) redirect reusable, safe and clean waste products from landfill and redistribute them to the wider community. For a list of stores see www.reusefuluk.org.

learning successfully, engage with the experience, discover and learn new words and phrases, find out about other cultures and traditions, enjoy a positive outcome and feel success – knowing and believing that they can do it.

Here are some tips and reminders for ensuring success when working with learners with SEND/ALN:

● Be consistent with routines and lesson starts.

● Establish ground rules and non-negotiables.

● Be clear and concise when giving instructions, and take the time to dual code them.

● Check that your learner is on board with you and understands the nature of task.

● Model what you are expecting (WAGOLL).

● Draw out written and spoken examples from the learners.

● Wear a microphone and speak clearly and slowly so the learners who need it can hear you (and don't forget you're wearing it!).

● Allow learners with speech difficulties to capture spoken work on a digital device.

● Limit long reading tasks if the learners struggle with this; instead, break down lengthy texts and share them out among the group. Be very mindful of individual's reading ages and use decoding strategies to make international language texts more accessible.

● Avoid setting too many writing tasks for learners with limited dexterity/mobility issues.

● Link new learning to prior learning and experiences, and then build on it.

- Use edtech appropriately to assist learning.

- Ensure that printed resources and materials are fully accessible.

- Don't forget to assess and give feedback for tasks completed using alternative formats rather than in exercise books.

- Allow learners to choose 'optimal learning partners' rather than working alone or with their TA. Friendships come and go but learners also like to swap and change.

- Monitor noise levels and the volume of your voice.

- Always have the necessary chargers to hand to keep essential electronic devices functioning for learners who need them.

- Record vocabulary items, key phrases and chunks of grammar using Apple Clips or a simple voice recording app or device. This means the learners do not have to continually read text to learn, plus they can access the content outside of the lesson.

- Consider the learning through more than one sense: not only to have a powerful impact on the learners but also so it is more memorable – and therefore more 'sticky'.

- Always have a back-up plan/activity, as well as an enrichment and extension task, to provide deeper discovery, stretch and challenge.

- Provide opportunities for reflection – for checking that a concept has been learned or a task completed to the best of the student's ability.

- Always have spare resources.

- Always check with your TA to ensure that your expectations for the learner are appropriate.

- Communicate with the learner and home, especially to celebrate successes and when challenges have been overcome.

- Never assume that all young people with SEND/ALN are the same; everyone is unique, as are their learning needs. Find out and understand what these are to help learners achieve to the best of their ability in your classroom.

NINE PRACTICAL IDEAS TO USE WITH LEARNERS WITH SEND/ALN

1. PUPPET SHOW

Finger puppets, marionettes and glove puppets are a brilliant tool for learners with SEND/ALN. They not only encourage students to speak, but they can also be used in class to dramatise the new language.

2. BREAK IT DOWN TO BUILD IT UP

Use Lego, building blocks or bricks – or create your own language jigsaws – to help learners to create sentence structures. Paper chains can be great for this too, although it will depend on your learners' dexterity. If you have the funds, check out Kloo (https://kloogame.com) which is a brilliant card game to aid with sentence-building, word order and cognition.

3. TONGUE-TWISTERS

Develop learners' confidence when speaking by creating a bank of one-line tongue-twisters. These can be devised to practise specific graphemes and phonemes or to include new vocabulary and phrases.

4. I GO, YOU GO

Practise turn-taking by passing, rolling or throwing an object around the room. Only the holder of the ball/soft toy/microphone (sparkly ones are my preference; one colleague had an inflatable microphone!) can answer. Depending on the size of your class you might need more than one item.

5. GET ACTIVE

Sitting behind a desk every lesson can be tough, so create opportunities for the students to be active in their language learning. Perhaps they could go to another room where there is more space. If it is possible them to go outside, you could chalk out hopscotch or place hula hoops and get them to practise colours, numbers, addition, subtraction, time, school subjects, likes and dislikes, and so on. Many aspects of language can be recalled and reinforced through active learning.

6. TO THE KITCHEN

If the students are learning about food, why not teach them how to cook? Crêpes, tarte flambée, croque-monsieur/croque-madame, Bratwurst, Currywurst, Schnitzel, Flammkuchen, patatas bravas, tacos or tortillas are great to introduce and cook with learners. Not only do the students get an opportunity to work in a kitchen environment, following a recipe, preparing and cooking a snack, followed by a luscious tasting experience, but they also gain a rich and memorable international language experience.

7. TOWN CLASSROOM CORNER

Create a shop, ticket office or other transactional situation in your classroom to help learners develop their language and life skills by selecting and purchasing items with money (the toy variety!). Cardboard shop fronts are easily available and aren't too expensive, but if you have a local scrapstore, time and a creative vision you could easily craft a doctor's/dentist's surgery, post office, tourist information bureau, fruit and veg stall or bakery as a setting for learners to practise speaking in another language and develop confidence in important life skills.

8. LET'S SING

Learning new sounds, words, phrases and grammar can be made so much easier if they are presented and learned alongside a song. There are many suitable foreign language songs out there, so it's worth checking out what is available online. You can also find videos on YouTube and other websites, although always check the lyrics and visuals carefully for suitability. Once the students have learned the song and the language, it can be recalled and used in other areas, reinforcing the transferability of vocabulary, phrases and grammar.

9. DO YOU CLIL?

There are lots of CLIL projects available through the British Council which connect classrooms, and the young people in them, across the globe. Of course there is the ELAPSE (Embedding Language Across Primary and Secondary Education) project, which has been funded by Erasmus+, researching and seeking to empower all teachers to adopt a CLIL approach across five countries. A more modern approach to pen pals (I'm thinking of my own unforgettable experiences from the 1980s), CLIL harnesses the technology we have in our classrooms to create brilliant language and cultural experiences that learners adore. There is a section on CLIL in Chapter 9 with 57 project ideas, although I'm sure you could come up with many of your own too.

MFL IN ALTERNATIVE PROVISION SETTINGS

Alternative provision (AP)[5] and its appropriateness for the young people it serves is currently very much under the microscope, which is no bad thing. I'm not going to wade into this discussion, but I do have concerns regarding young people's access to international languages, and the quality of that provision, in AP settings. From my own limited experience of AP, I'm aware that decisions are made to ensure the curriculum is appropriate for the students, but often this is limited to 'core' subjects, usually English, maths, science, life skills and PE, and possibly expressive arts and music. Languages provision is limited beyond

---

5   Alternative provision takes place outside of schools for learners who are unable to access mainstream education. The reasons for this can be varied and wide-ranging, including behavioural issues, exclusion, illness or school refusal.

mastering English and support for learners with English as an additional language, with few AP settings offering access to an international language. Communication is an increasingly important life skill, so learning a second language can only be an added bonus. It has been said that learners adopt and express different personality traits in different languages. People who are fluent in more than one language and the associated cultural frameworks even seem to change personality as they change language.[6] This point is reinforced by Freda Mishan who observes that learning a second language gives learners the sensation that they have different personality traits and are a 'different person' in the international language.[7]

Understandably, in many AP settings the priority is the well-being and safety of young people who may have had adverse life experiences and limited experience of a positive and stable education. From the outset, forming a connection with the individual, accepting them for who they are without judgement, and building trust, confidence, self-esteem and a feeling of safety is paramount. The desire for students to engage and experience progress can take time; it can be like a rollercoaster for those individuals who have had negative educational experiences or who have felt ostracised

---

6   See D. Luna, T. Ringberg and L. A. Peracchio, One Individual, Two Identities: Frame Switching among Biculturals, *Journal of Consumer Research* 35(2) (2008): 279–293. Available at: https://www.researchgate.net/publication/23547452_One_Individual_Two_Identities_Frame_Switching_among_Biculturals; F. Grosjean, Change of Language, Change of Personality?, *Psychology Today* (1 November 2011). Available at: https://www.psychologytoday.com/gb/blog/life-bilingual/201111/change-language-change-personality; N. Prentis, Feel More Fun in French? Your Personality Can Change Depending on the Language You Speak, *Quartz* (8 March 2017). Available at: https://qz.com/925630/feel-more-fun-in-french-your-personality-can-change-depending-on-the-language-you-speak.

7   F. Mishan, *Designing Authenticity into Language Learning Materials* (Bristol: Intellect, 2005).

through exclusion. Alongside the support the young person requires, language learning can add stability, a different and positive perspective, and feelings of achievement and success. The benefits include:

- A positive boost to self-esteem.
- Improved communication skills.
- Increased knowledge and reinforcement of understanding of first/native language.
- Enhanced receptive skills.
- Improved production skills and quality of learner output.
- Horizons extended beyond the learner's current experiences.
- Different lifestyles and perspectives are promoted.
- Increased understanding of other languages, countries, cultures and traditions, promoting tolerance.
- Access to a subject experience not previously possessed.
- Improved cognition and oracy.
- Extended vocabulary range.
- Increased cultural capital and awareness.
- Improved life chances and employability.
- Resilience and persistence are promoted in a safe, risk-free setting.

We need to look beyond the historic definition of what is 'core' and build a more expansive curriculum for learners in AP settings. Of course, it is important to consider teacher expertise to assure students of a good-quality learning experience. I hope that the experiential learning and CLIL approaches described in this chapter, and throughout the book, might aid discussion about a more inclusive and robust approach to international language learning and provision.

CHAPTER 9

WHY IS MFL A SUBJECT WORTH TEACHING?

MFL AND THE SECONDARY CURRICULUM

The introduction of languages to the curriculum in every comprehensive school across the UK in the second half of the 20th century was nothing short of a triumph for every child born thereafter. Languages were no longer reserved for students attending independent, private and grammar schools, but were accessible to all across the full ability range for the first time. The new CSE and O level qualifications reflected this important shift, which meant that children like me, from working-class families, could learn a second language.

Sadly, the support for languages is now in decline, as evidenced through:

- The demise of compulsory language learning in 2011.

- The abolition of critical advisory services and centres of research for language learning in 2010.

- Schools failing to offer language lessons to students across the full ability and age range.

- The decline in the allocation of language lessons at a range of levels.

- The decline in the breadth of languages available in sixth forms and universities.

- Half the population of the UK seeing limited value in the UK's membership of the European Union.

To mention just a few. That said, the introduction of the English Baccalaureate (EBacc)[1] has shown that there is support for the continuation of languages in England, but not all schools follow the EBacc route. This is despite the government aspiration that by 2025, 90% of young people in England should leave secondary education with a GCSE in a foreign language.[2] In 2018 the Department for Education launched MFL hub schools and have committed millions of pounds to developing excellence in language pedagogy as a direct result of the *Modern Foreign Languages Pedagogy Review*.[3] As this is a very new development, I will be following closely, like many other MFL practitioners. I hope the research, resources and pedagogic approach to languages teaching will be freely available to all schools, not just the hub schools, and have clear links to supporting primary and secondary languages learning and provision. The programme is well funded, so I am hoping this initiative will have a positive and tangible impact on language learning across the UK, and will not be shelved prematurely.

---

1   The English Baccalaureate was introduced in England in 2017 and measures the percentage of students who achieve five or more 5–9 grades in traditional academic GCSE subjects: English, maths, two sciences, a foreign language and history or geography.

2   House of Commons Library, Language Teaching in Schools (England). Briefing Paper 07388 (16 October 2019), p. 3. Available at: https://researchbriefings. parliament.uk/ResearchBriefing/Summary/CBP-7388.

3   I. Bauckham, *Modern Foreign Languages Pedagogy Review: A Review of Modern Foreign Languages Teaching Practice in Key Stage 3 and Key Stage 4* (Teaching Schools Council, 2016). Available at: https://pureyork.ac.uk/portal/ files/54043904/MFL_Pedagogy_Review_Report_TSC_PUBLISHED_VERSION_ Nov_2016_1_.pdf.

The future of languages is at a critical point, one that has been coming for a number of years. Languages teachers across all sectors are acutely aware of this, so they are grateful for the work of the British Council, Teresa Tinsley and colleagues who, since 2002, have analysed annual data collected from thousands of state and independent schools who complete the *Language Trends* survey.[4] The survey is a detailed analysis of trends within languages teaching and assesses the impact of educational policy in relation to languages in schools. It is a shame that out of the 32,770 schools registered in England[5] at the time of writing not all find the time to complete it, although over 2,000 teachers do. Some of the key questions it asks address:

- Exam entries, changes and statistics.

- Reduction of Key Stage 3 to two years.

- Recruitment and retention of languages teachers.

- Provision, range and uptake for the big three languages plus heritage and ancient languages.

- Primary languages.

- Post-16.

- Concerns for languages teachers.

The All-Party Parliamentary Group (APPG) on Modern Languages was created in 2014 following significant concerns from politicians, linguists and other interested parties, such as the British Council and the Association for Language Learning (www.all-languages.org.uk), for whom

---

4   T. Tinsley, *Language Trends 2019: Language Teaching in Primary and Secondary Schools in England. Survey Report* (London: British Council, 2019). Available at: https://www.britishcouncil.org/research-policy-insight/research-reports/language-trends-2019.

5   See https://www.besa.org.uk/key-uk-education-statistics.

languages are extremely important. In March 2019, the group published their National Recovery Programme for Languages, a framework proposal to address the dramatic decline in languages provision across the UK and the impact of the UK's languages deficit economically, socially and culturally.[6] The framework outlines the group's vision as well as five strategic objectives to achieve a step change in the UK's languages capability for schools, further and higher education, business, industry, government and society. This is a welcome document which has the support of many languages teachers and educational associations. The vision, goals and aspirations need a wider audience – and support from government, head teachers and senior leaders – in order for there to be a significant boost to children's language learning experiences in schools.

It's not impossible to build a curriculum around international languages (the CLIL movement in schools promotes just this), although learning geography, history, science, music, art and the range of technology subjects through the medium of a language is becoming increasingly rare. This is an unfortunate consequence of the specialisms of qualified teaching staff and the increase in accountability measures in schools, such as Progress 8 and Attainment 8 in England. Pressures on time, the newly introduced 'more rigorous' A level in 2016 and GCSE in 2018 in England, school policies, timetabling constraints, decreases in funding and lack of language specialists also contribute to the problem. However, I am certain that CLIL has much to offer.

---

6   All-Party Parliamentary Group on Modern Languages, A National Recovery
    Programme for Languages: A Framework Proposal from the All-Party
    Parliamentary Group on Modern Languages (4 March 2019). Available at:
    https://secure.toolkitfiles.co.uk/clients/34124/sitedata/files/A-national-
    recovery-programme-for-languages.pdf.

There seems to be less time allocated to teaching languages experientially through project-based learning, with a focus instead on a more rigid and restricted rote schedule of study. CLIL requires teachers to have a subject specialism in at least two fields, or for subject teachers who are also passionate linguists to have the proficiency to teach both subjects. There is support out there for lovers of CLIL through the British Council, and also from the aforementioned ELAPSE project, and British International Schools overseas do this daily through the medium of English, preparing for their learners to complete the iGCSE, A levels or the International Baccalaureate (IB).

An increasing number of schools are opting for the 'knowledge organiser curriculum' as a method for language learning (i.e. a curriculum built around knowledge organisers). Potentially, the result of this trend is learners who are adept in a narrower range of language across topics, rather than the relatively diverse range within programmes of study or the deeper learning characterised by the experiential CLIL approach. Well-crafted knowledge organisers which recycle language and structures can be a positive addition to the MFL classroom, providing these are carefully constructed to support schemes of learning. However, in my experience this is not always the case for MFL. Curriculums should be built around the learners and the local community, providing a high-quality, broad and balanced education. This is vital if learners are going to have the best possible start in life, through learning about themselves, developing knowledge and skills, and seeing positive role models who reflect themselves and others in their community, while also raising aspirations and having the highest of expectations through well-designed resources and experiences. The curriculum should be developed with all learners in mind, and appropriately crafted with the necessary support, scaffolding, enrichment and extension.

There is significant debate as to whether curriculums should be knowledge based (or knowledge rich) or skills based. I find this astounding: how can a languages curriculum or lesson *not* be knowledge rich? In order for learners to become confident and competent linguists who can communicate successfully with confidence, fluency and clarity with native speakers, they need to be clear on the propositional knowledge (grammar, word order, pronunciation rules, grapheme–phoneme links, facts about the countries where the language is used and those countries' cultures, traditions, people, festivals and celebrations) as well as the procedural knowledge (how and when to use tenses and grammar rules, how to construct a sentence applying grammar rules, how to pronounce words in an international language, when pronunciation rules should be applied and when there are exceptions).

Languages classrooms in the UK and across the globe educate and inspire linguists to be able to decode, understand, process and synthesise. The aim is for students to be able to correctly use an international language through spoken and written language skills, to visit other countries to live and work, and to embrace new cultures by immersing themselves in a different way of life. All of this cannot be achieved without knowledge *and* skills. Someone could have all of the linguistic propositional knowledge ever conceived about a language, but it would be useless if they were unable to apply it. Would they be able to communicate successfully? I doubt it. Equally, to be a competent linguist we need to have a good understanding of propositional knowledge, and not just be highly competent at listening, speaking, reading and writing.

CONTENT AND LANGUAGE INTEGRATED LEARNING

Many schools in Wales teach through the medium of the Welsh language, and I was delighted to see this in action at Ysgol Gyfun Gymraeg Bro Edern in Cardiff. Like other Welsh-medium schools, Bro Edern serves its city and teaches students of all abilities in this way, in the same way as many international schools where language acquisition has been pushed to the fore. All students experience learning through a language other than English, which helps to promote internationalism, global thinking, empathy and tolerance, while also developing and nurturing a lifelong love of language.

The CLIL approach to learning and education is an aspiration for some, but it is already happening on a smaller scale in Wales. The new draft Curriculum for Wales, which will be used from 2022, has merged MFL with Welsh and English under the banner of 'Language, Literacy and Communication',[7] which encompasses all international languages and will be one of six areas of experience. I look forward to seeing the impact of the new Curriculum for Wales on engagement, motivation and progress, as well as its effect on the uptake in languages.

Cross-curricular programmes and projects focused on common aspects across a range of subjects provide opportunities for deep and enriching learning experiences on a smaller scale, providing that staff are willing and have the necessary subject expertise to collaborate in this way. Let's take, for example, the GCSE International and Global Dimension theme and within this 'environmental issues, being green and access to natural resources': there is a real

---

7   See https://hwb.gov.wales/draft-curriculum-for-wales-2022/languages-literacy-and-communication.

scope here for meaningful collaboration with environmental scientists in the science or geography teams to further inspire students to take action about the climate crisis. Young people are increasingly speaking out thanks to the call to arms from Greta Thunberg, the Swedish school student and climate activist whose Skolstrejk för klimatet (School Strike for the Climate) has become a global phenomenon. When a brave and passionate young voice speaks out – the message ricocheting across the world, inspiring peers as well as politicians – as teachers we cannot ignore it. We have to act on this awareness, passion and action, and capitalise on it in the classroom.

CLIL projects, which are creative and invite curiosity, hook learners in through a wide range of subjects and topics, while also acknowledging the skills and knowledge required for terminal assessments as well as, and perhaps more importantly, for real life beyond educational institutions. Global projects provide additional support for universal thinking and internationalism, which takes learners beyond their immediate surroundings. The collaborative approach also fosters closer connections between departments and staff groups through opportunities to pool resources, provide in-house CPD and share teachers' skills, knowledge and ideas. In addition to highlighting for students the overlap in skills, knowledge and understanding across different subject areas, CLIL projects also promote the transference of specific knowledge, which forges stronger links across subjects/topics and reinforces familiarity and expertise. Recall of memories and information favours abstract and memorable learning experiences – and what can be more unforgettable than a collaborative cross-curricular project? CLIL and other partnerships offer positive and enriching experiences for students, so they should be something that all schools consider.

The forthcoming 2024 Summer Olympics, which is to be held in France, is a perfect opportunity to excite learners through a PE and language team collaboration. Similarly, the devastating fire at Notre-Dame in 2019, which ripped through the medieval Gothic cathedral, provides scope for a collaboration between technology and language teams. Both projects could be linked through the GCSE themes of Future Aspirations, Study and Work, or the International and Global Dimension themes on projects with global prominence, or, of course, the more obvious themes of Local Area, Holiday and Travel or Identity and Culture. I'm describing the Edexcel framework here as that is what my school uses, but I'm sure you can see how this could be made applicable to the specification that your school follows, if from a different exam board.

On pages 190–198 you wll find ten CLIL opportunities based on the five Edexcel GCSE themes and 57 cross-curricular project ideas.

Theme	Sub-themes	CLIL project ideas	Subject teams	Others
		Tackling the climate crisis		
International and Global Dimension	Environmental issues Bringing the world together	1 Raising the profile of the impact of global heating 2 Arranging a demonstration 3 Organising travel to and from the event 4 Feeding the world sustainably 5 Alternative sustainable solutions to big global problems	Geography, science, MFL	Philosophy, sociology, pastoral and tutor groups, PSHE
		2024 Paris Olympics		
International and Global Dimension Identity and Culture Future Aspirations, Study and Work	Bringing the world together Who am I? Daily life Cultural life	1 Fitness and lifestyle – who am I? 2 Diet, fitness and activity 3 Aspirations for the future 4 Food, well-being and lifestyle	PE, media studies, science, food technology, business studies, MFL	Philosophy, pastoral and tutor groups, PSHE

		Refugees, migration and me		
Identity and Culture	Who am I?	1 Who am I? – my story	English, history, media studies, art, music, drama, dance, PE, MFL	Philosophy, pastoral and tutor groups, PSHE
Local Area, Holiday and Travel	Daily life	2 Where am I from and where will I go?		
Future Aspirations, Study and Work	Cultural life	3 Welcoming a new student to the school		
	School	4 Volunteering in a refugee centre		
	School activities	5 Arranging a charitable event		
	Town, region and country	6 Celebrating unity – coming together and celebrating cultures, traditions and customs		
	Using languages beyond the classroom			
	Volunteering	5 Tackling inactivity in young people		
	Work	6 Arranging a charity sporting event		
		Using languages beyond the classroom		

Theme	Sub-themes	CLIL project ideas	Subject teams	Others
		Rebuilding Notre-Dame de Paris		
Identity and Culture Local Area, Holiday and Travel Future Aspirations, Study and Work	Who am I? Daily life Cultural life Holidays Travel and tourist transactions Town, region and country Using languages beyond the classroom Ambitions Work	1 Campaign to raise the funds to rebuild Notre-Dame 2 Volunteering to assist in the rebuild 3 Press report to raise the profile of an event 4 Why is Notre-Dame so important? 5 Restore or redesign – what would you do?	Technology, art, music, drama, ICT, media, history, RE, maths, philosophy, science, MFL	English, pastoral and tutor groups, PSHE

International Women's Day

Identity and Culture	Who am I?	1 Celebrating the achievements of women	Whole school	Philosophy, pastoral and tutor groups, PSHE
Future Aspirations, Study and Work	Daily life	2 Fighting for global equality		
International and Global Dimension	Cultural life	3 Using our voices – using your vote		
	Using languages beyond the classroom	4 Education for girls		
	Ambitions	5 Wonderful women of our time		
	Work			
	Bringing the world together			

Unity Day

Identity and Culture	Who am I?	1 Celebrating unity – coming together and celebrating cultures, traditions and customs	Art, music, drama, dance, PE, ICT, English, history, RE	Pastoral and tutor groups, PSHE, citizenship
School	Daily life	2 Education for all		
Future Aspirations, Study and Work	Cultural life	3 Tolerance for all		
International and Global Dimension	What school is like			
	School activities			

Theme	Sub-themes	CLIL project ideas	Subject teams	Others
	Using languages beyond the classroom Ambitions Work Bringing the world together	4 Breaking down barriers – embracing our neighbours 5 Festivals and celebrations	philosophy, sociology, science, technology, media studies, business studies, MFL	
		#Envision2030 United Nations Global Goals		
Identity and Culture Local Area, Holiday and Travel School Future Aspirations, Study and Work	Who am I? Daily life Cultural life Holidays Travel and tourist transactions	1 Poverty and hunger 2 School, education and me 3 Sustainable cities and communities 4 Humanity vs the world 5 Gender equality	Whole school	Pastoral and tutor groups

		Festivals and celebrations		
Identity and Culture	Who am I?	1 Karneval, Carnival and Mardi Gras	Art, music, drama, dance, English,	ICT
Local Area, Holiday and Travel	Daily life	2 Halloween/All Hallows' Eve and El Día de los Muertos		
Future Aspirations, Study and Work	Cultural life			
	Holidays			
	Town, region and country	6 Diversity		
	What school is like	7 Life on land – life below water		
International and Global Dimension	School activities			
	Using languages beyond the classroom			
	Ambitions			
	Work			
	Bringing the world together			
	Environmental issues			

Theme	Sub-themes	CLIL project ideas	Subject teams	Others
International and Global Dimension	Travel and tourist transactions Town, region and country Using languages beyond the classroom Ambitions Work Bringing the world together	3 Benicàssim, Rock am Ring, Montreal and the global music festival scene 4 Puppetry, giants and storytelling 5 Eurovision	media studies, technology, RE, MFL	
		The arts		
Identity and Culture Local Area, Holiday and Travel	Who am I? Daily life Cultural life	1 Music around the globe 2 Art's timeless impact 3 Global literary voices from the trenches	Art, music, drama, dance, PE, English,	ICT, pastoral and tutor groups

				Pastoral and tutor groups
Future Aspirations, Study and Work International and Global Dimension	Holidays Travel and tourist transactions Town, region and country Using languages beyond the classroom Ambitions Work Bringing the world together	4 Fantastic foreign language films 5 Fairy tales by the Brothers Grimm 6 Storytelling – students crafting their own stories and language 7 Performance poetry slam	history, media studies, MFL	
Identity and Culture School Future Aspirations, Study and Work	Who am I? Daily life Cultural life What school is like	**Technology** 1 Technology and me – the impact on my well-being 2 Transformative technology – why is technology so amazing? 3 Technology for all	ICT, media studies, technology, philosophy, sociology, MFL	

Theme	Sub-themes	CLIL project ideas	Subject teams	Others
International and Global Dimension	School activities Using languages beyond the classroom Ambitions Work Bringing the world together Environmental issues	4 Building websites – from coding to communication 5 The cost of technology on humans and the planet 6 Is the cost of technology too high?		

The key is to not miss amazing real-life opportunities to rethink the big picture and to enrich the languages classroom and learning journey for students. Bringing (appropriate) world events to the classroom experience helps learners to feel part of the global solution, boosts motivation and engagement, and deepens their knowledge of the world. The impact will be seen in language lessons and in the classrooms of other subject teams with whom you collaborate – everyone benefits. These types of projects inspire curiosity, awaken the senses and help to foster thinking on real solutions to real-life problems. They also help learners to see how subject knowledge is transferable, while also improving recall and reinforcing and building on their prior knowledge. Furthermore, we are developing confident young people who can work collaboratively and creatively across a range of subjects to solve problems and challenges.

When collaborative cross-curricular learning happens successfully, different subject teams come together to define precisely what they want the students to learn, what skills student linguists need to develop and what social, emotional, life and learning skills must be cultivated. Once clarified, the subject teams can identify common themes and subjects (e.g. morphology (grammar), etymology and syntax) and skill development (e.g. grapheme–phoneme links, oracy, listening, decoding to access reading, literacy, collaborative group work, creative thinking, problem/challenge-based learning, design thinking, product design, curiosity, creativity, performance art) to design a student-centric curriculum which builds and strengthens knowledge and purpose.

The student-centric approach means that all learners are catered for without exception, not just those in specific groups or bands. Commonality supports students' knowledge, language skills, social skills and understanding, as well as their confidence, competence, fluency and, of course, progress. As they advance through subject-specific content, it is more deeply understood by being reinforced across multiple subjects, in both native and international languages.

It is unfortunate that this type of approach is uncommon in schools, because as well as being fantastic for learners it also supports peer collaboration among teachers, developing deeper pedagogic understanding about how other subjects are taught and sequenced. Cooperation with teachers from other subject areas also offers the benefits of in-house CPD, subject curriculum design and improved cross-curricular appreciation. This can pave the way for diverse thinking which can inspire and enrich the language curriculum when the next phase of monitoring, evaluation and review is discussed within the languages team.

When you next review your language curriculum, ask the following questions and answer them honestly:

- What is it like to be a student in your classroom?

- What are the students learning and is it useful?

- How do we know they are learning it, and where can they show what they know?

- Are they enjoying their language learning? What is the evidence?

- Are there frequent opportunities for the students to be creative with the language they have secured and are learning?

- How are the students being developed to become skilful and confident orators, listeners, readers and writers through the international language?

- What do the students say about the subject/language lessons/curriculum, and what are we going to do about it?

- Are we taking all the students with us on the learning journey? If we aren't, how are we going to address this?

- If the students were parachuted into [a country], would they be able to have a conversation?

- Are we exposing students to overseas culture, art, music, drama, destinations, food, lifestyles, festivals, celebrations and traditions?

- What do we need to do differently to engage all our students in language learning?

- How does our languages curriculum prepare students for life beyond school, beyond the UK and to compete on an international scale?

- Do specific groups of learners achieve as well as other learners in language lessons across the subject team and across the school?

- What can we learn from the *Modern Foreign Languages Pedagogy Review* and other MFL research to enhance the languages experience for our learners? And what are we actually doing about it?

The secondary languages curriculum faces various challenges, including the increased drive for a two-year Key Stage 3 to cope with the additional rigour of the new GCSEs, which places increased pressure on the coverage of the programmes of study. This, in turn, could result in surface learning rather than a deeper exploration of topics, grammar and language alongside exposure to different cultures and traditions through real-life learning, all of which provides opportunities for students to make their own connections. If international languages are worth teaching, they have to be worth learning. This translates as MFL and language learning having authentic outcomes via creative, engaging and inclusive cultural experiences which expose students to a range of language, grammar, topics, songs, music, drama and art, while also developing all four language skills and promoting curiosity.

Speaking and oracy activities must have a genuine purpose. Are learners speaking to young French people or creating written pieces to email or post to Spanish friends overseas? Are listening experiences filled with authentic language spoken by people with whom they can identify and connect? Do reading texts contain original dialogue – modern themes and phrases used by young people overseas? Or are we simply giving them textbook tasks and past paper questions? Of course, some resources will need to be adapted, but if students know they are using realia and genuine sources, they will engage more and put extra effort and focus into their output.

Of course, our primary colleagues can assist us with this, providing we work with them.

MFL AND THE PRIMARY CURRICULUM

Language teaching and learning was introduced into UK primary schools in the 1990s with modern languages in the primary school (MLPS), and more formally with the introduction of the 2013 Languages Programmes of Study for Key Stage 2, which provided primary colleagues with additional direction, support, key topics, vocabulary and grammar.[8] The aspiration for the languages programme was to place languages firmly within the primary curriculum, but according to Teresa Tinsley and Neela Doležal, the disparity between provision, expertise and contact has resulted in some primary teachers reporting that language teaching is a 'marginal subject' which is 'challenging to deliver alongside many other competing demands'.[9] Data shared at the transition stage can ease learners' progression from Key Stage 2 to Key Stage 3 in some subjects, but this is not the case for language teaching. Tinsley and Doležal also state that primary colleagues cite 'limited contact' with secondary colleagues as a huge issue, and there are concerns that some secondary teachers disregard primary language learning data as 'inconsistent' and the progress recorded as minimal. This is shame because collaboration with primary colleagues benefits both learners and secondary language specialists. By not acknowledging children's primary languages experience, there is also the matter of de-skilling learners who have had a high-quality experience.

There are those who dismiss primary languages provision as being all about song and little else, but this is simply untrue in many schools. There are some amazing primary language practitioners out there who create meaningful and enriching learning experiences, including a range of vocabulary, grammar and transferable language. Primary linguists work hard to connect with one another through organisations such as the Association for Language

---

8 Department for Education, *Languages Programmes of Study: Key Stage 2 National Curriculum in England* (September 2013). Ref: DFE-00174-2013. Available at: https://assets.publishing.service.gov.uk/government/uploads/system/uploads/attachment_data/file/239042/PRIMARY_national_curriculum_-_Languages.pdf.

9 T. Tinsley and N. Doležal, *Language Trends 2018: Language Teaching in Primary and Secondary Schools in England. Survey Report* (London: British Council, 2018), p. 3. Available at: https://www.britishcouncil.org/sites/default/files/language_trends_2018_report.pdf.

Learning and Twitter (#MFLTwitterati) and Facebook (Languages in Primary Schools), resulting in incredible curriculum programmes and experiential learning.

This is not to say that there aren't things we could be doing better. We are perhaps not making sufficient learning links between primary and secondary to ease transition. Whether this is a problem with the creation or the receipt of data, it can result in disconnection and repetition. Assumptions are made about a perceived lack of languages work, and so secondary colleagues start from scratch. Valuable evidence of prior attainment needs to be shared, as well as any qualitative information gathered by languages teachers from feeder schools. This would result in a more connected and continuous experience for both learners and teachers.

How many secondary teachers connect with feeder primary schools and read through their languages programmes of study? Likewise, do primary colleagues know the first elements of Key Stage 3 programmes of study? A better understanding of the learning journey from Key Stages 2 and 3 through to Key Stages 4 and 5, as well as greater dialogue, will lead to higher levels of student engagement, motivation, skill development and aptitude, and perhaps achievement.

This is not a criticism of schools, merely an observation. All teachers are busy, no one is disputing that, but there is a missed opportunity here which impacts on learners' motivation and progress. Of course, where a secondary school has a small languages team and more than 30 feeder primary schools this would be a huge additional burden. Perhaps one benefit of the rise of multi-academy trusts will be greater consistency across learners' linguistic journeys – we shall see.

A colleague worked across primary and secondary as a very successful MFL teacher. She created and delivered a high-quality German curriculum in primary schools in the South West using the wealth of resources and ideas on the Goethe-Institut website.[10] She crafted meaningful lessons centred around the adventures of Felix and Franzi, two puppets who would regularly make an appearance in her classroom.[11] The students were engaged and excited, not least because this lesson was taught by a visiting teacher, which added an element of intrigue. She worked with their usual class teacher to link the learning to the pro-grammes of study, while also making her lessons a very progressive and engaging languages experience.[12]

She had high expectations, and the learners responded with their own research into Germany, the German lan-guage, and historical and familial connections. Engage-ment was superb and attitudes to learning were extremely positive. The learners would run up to her as she entered the school (or if they bumped into her in the shops around town with their families), speaking sentence-level German and asking questions perfectly. These children went off to secondary school with two solid years of language learn-ing under their belt, so it was frustrating to discover that some secondary colleagues weren't interested in the pro-gress they had made and chose to 'restart' their language learning in Year 7.

I also know of a language storytelling project in primary schools across parts of South Wales which has reinforced the children's love of *The Gruffalo* through the medium of German.[13] It has had a fantastic impact not only on the learners' German but also on their reading skills and oracy.

---

10 See https://www.goethe.de/ins/gb/en/spr/unt/kum.html.

11 See https://www.goethe.de/ins/gb/en/spr/unt/kum/dfk/dff.html.

12 See Department for Education, *Languages Programmes of Study: Key Stage 2.*

13 See https://www.all-languages.org.uk/features/the-gruffalo-in-german.

There are many projects out there connecting primary classrooms with languages, and placing children and their love of stories, sports and other hobbies at the heart of it all. Secondary colleagues simply must communicate more with primary colleagues to find out about their great work and build on it, rather than dismiss it. The transition from primary to secondary is extremely stressful for learners and their families, so anything that we can do to ease this will benefit the well-being and progress of individual learners.

TEN WAYS TO IMPROVE TRANSITION FROM THE PRIMARY LANGUAGES CLASSROOM TO SECONDARY

1   Connect with colleagues at least twice per year if possible (in the spring and summer terms). Diarise this to make sure it happens. One meeting could take place in each school, with an agenda of points to provide a focus for discussion.

2   If you are a secondary teacher, make time to learn more about attainment and progress in feeder schools by visiting and supporting primary MFL colleagues.

3   Work collaboratively to identify, collate and share key information to best support learners in making the transition from Key Stage 2 to Key Stage 3.

4   Be clear on the overlap in vocabulary, language and grammar between Key Stages 2 and 3.

5   Secondary teachers should consider how prior learning can be built on to deepen knowledge and reinforce language learning through retrieval tasks.

6   Identify key information to share to best support learners' continued progress and language skills attainment.

7   Create or adopt a joint project to enable primary language learners to show what they know and are capable of, and invite secondary colleagues to a celebration, graduation or languages meet event. This could also be attended by parents/carers to celebrate their child's language achievements to date.

8   Share the identified data/language information in an easy-to-access format. Secondary teachers can use this to create 'expert linguists' in the Year 7 languages classroom to ease the worries of peers who may not have had any previous languages input.

9   Consider carefully whether a restart is actually required. This can be incredibly demotivating for learners who may well have had several years of language learning experience.

10 Some secondary schools have as many as 50 feeder schools, so the chances of visiting all of them are slim. Instead, secondary colleagues could host an event for their primary colleagues to share information and forge stronger links.

Mutually acknowledging and valuing one another's professionalism and contributions, as well as connecting, can only serve to improve transition in MFL. Some schools do this brilliantly, but barriers such as the pressures on time, Key Stage 2 SATs, the reduction in gained time and increasing demand on finances can lead to challenges. When transition is done well, learners flourish and make positive leaps forward in languages, building on the firm foundations created in Key Stage 2, especially when some students will be constructing sentences and paragraphs using more than one tense and clearly benefitting from a collaborative and sequential approach. There is no quick fix to getting transition right, but since the demise of local county language network coordinators (who supported both primary and secondary colleagues), the Association for Language Learning (ALL) has collated some valuable information – including research, case studies and reports – to help primary colleagues get their learners ready for secondary school.[14] This can be shared with learners, parents, carers, governors and other stakeholders, as well as with secondary colleagues.

As well as lots of bloggers in this area, there is also the recent Research in Primary Languages report,[15] which can help to support and further boost the great work and aspirations of our primary colleagues to develop quality language learning and a robust languages curriculum for all. Perhaps digital hangout platforms and applications such as Skype and Zoom could be used to organise meetings that forge relationships and facilitate a more continuous languages learning experience for students. We ignore the work of primary languages colleagues at our peril. If you are a secondary teacher and you aren't yet

---

14 Expert Subject Advisory Group - Modern Foreign Languages, *Assessment in Modern Foreign Languages in the Primary School* (January 2015). Available at: https://www.all-languages.org.uk/wp-content/uploads/2016/01/ESAGMFLGroupAssessmentStatement.pdf.

15 B. Holmes and F. Myles, *White Paper: Primary Languages Policy in England - The Way Forward* (Research in Primary Languages, 2019). Available at: http://www.ripl.uk/wp-content/uploads/2019/02/RIPL-White-Paper-Primary-Languages-Policy-in-England.pdf. A summary paper is available at: http://www.ripl.uk/wp-content/uploads/2019/08/HolmesMylesWhitePaperSummary.pdf.

aware of some great primary practitioners, please check out the following:

- @lisibo
- @valleseco
- @all4language
- @valelanguages
- Language Magician: www.thelanguagemagician.net
- Primary Languages Network: https://primarylanguages.network
- Sue Cave: www.cavelanguages.co.uk
- Languages in Primary Schools (LIPS): www.facebook.com/groups/primarylanguages

These are just some of the many individuals and organisations who are providing superb languages experiences and ideas for early years foundation stage (EYFS) and primary learners via websites and social media. When primary colleagues are this skilful, we must make sure that we prepare ourselves at secondary level for more than just *ab initio* learners coming into their first language lessons. In order to do this we have to become more familiar with the primary framework for languages and with what learners are expected to be able to do at Key Stage 2.

TEN WAYS TO CONTINUE LANGUAGE EXPERIENCES FOR CASH-STRAPPED SCHOOLS

1. CULTURAL CALENDAR

Download a global cultural calendar from one of the brilliant providers listed below, where you will also find additional links to resources and activities. Cultural calendars help to link learning and languages to international events and celebrations, which can also draw on the expertise of learners in the room and their families. Languages experiences should be about more than just cultural events, but it is a good start.

www.classtools.net/calendar.php

www.childmindingmatters.org.uk/forthcoming-festivals

www.timeanddate.com/holidays/world/world-religion-day

2. WHO DOES YOUR SCHOOL SERVE?

A wealth of cultural and linguistic riches are certain to be found local to your school, in the backgrounds of community members, in addition to that of the children who attend your school. Don't forget to 'activate' them to share their linguistic and cultural experiences to support a real-life languages encounter in the classroom. (Just check beforehand that this is OK with them and support any preparatory tasks.) Heritage languages are just as important as the international languages which are traditionally taught in schools. In addition, you could contact parents, carers, local businesses, government offices, museums, parks and tourist attractions and invite them in to share their understanding of international languages and cultural experiences. Obviously, there are safeguarding issues which would need to be addressed before welcoming visitors into the school, but this is a great way to make connections with the local community.

3. eTWINNING

Whether you are a primary or a secondary linguist, you and your learners can benefit from the opportunity to communicate, collaborate and develop shared projects via the eTwinning platform (www.etwinning.net). Colleagues rave about the projects they have worked on and the international connections they have made, and how this has opened up their classrooms and motivated learners not only to learn another language but also to enrich their knowledge of other cultures and promote tolerance. eTwinning is free to use and provides wonderful authentic learning experiences without the need to travel overseas. Colleagues can instead share their experiences via Skype, vlogs, emails, craft projects or even handwritten letters to help develop learners' written and oral confidence. Language and cultural exchange has an extremely positive effect on learners, which can only be a good thing! Note that this scheme may be affected by the UK's decision to leave the European Union.

4. SCOUR THE INTERNET

Every school in the UK has access to the internet, as do many overseas schools, so use it! Spend time investigating and seeking out the excellent digital languages resources that are out there, many of which are free to use (although be wary of poor-quality resources that contain errors or are potentially offensive). Investigate the sites I have highlighted in this book. This may take a while but it will be worth it. Just make sure that you set aside time for adaptation and/or differentiation.

5. CONNECT WITH LOCAL GROUPS

There are networks of languages teachers doing amazing things and sharing their expertise at events throughout the year. TeachMeets, local languages networks, primary/secondary hubs and education conferences are just a few events that are free. Seek these out and benefit from connecting with other schools and languages teachers. If you are in a rural school, why not link up with other schools online? Look out for feeder schools, city schools or schools with the same values as yours, contact them and find out what collaboration could bring to your classrooms. It could be the start of something truly beautiful! There are also ALL hubs in many areas, so pop along and see what they are doing too.

6. BBC LANGUAGES

Alongside BBC Bitesize, there is a wealth of free resources available from BBC Languages. Although this is an 'archived' site, and therefore no longer updated, it still contains a great deal of useful information for schools. It covers EYFS through to Key Stage 5, including Scottish Standard qualifications, across Chinese, French, German, Greek, Italian, Portuguese and Spanish (33 international languages are represented), at varying levels and depths.

There is lots to choose from and explore. Additional BBC Teach videos are available on YouTube.[16]

I am excited to learn that new BBC Bitesize resources will be launched in 2020, which will support language learning more authentically and in a more engaging way for all-through language learners.

www.bbc.co.uk/bitesize/subjects

www.bbc.co.uk/languages

7. INTERNATIONAL LANGUAGES TV CHANNELS

Stacks of information and language resources are available through native television channels. These tend to be focused at secondary, Key Stage 5 and further education levels, but they are freely available and packed with amazing news stories and videos of native speakers (with subtitles). Check out:

https://apprendre.tv5monde.com/fr

www.bbc.com/mundo

www.bbc.com/zhongwen/simp

www.daserste.de

www.s4c.cymru/en/education

8. LIVE LINGUA

Resources, downloads and eBooks are all available for free from Live Lingua. Although it is an international site it is easy to navigate. The range of resources differs depending on the language (the site has materials for over 100

---

16 See https://www.youtube.channel/UC4KN50fa17f45fx2DqG7ttg.

languages), but there is a strong emphasis on grammar. There are also videos and audio files of native speakers which are more suited to secondary, Key Stage 5 and further education language students.

www.livelingua.com

9. FluentU

Jakob Gibbons from FluentU has collated 49 free language learning websites for hard-up schools and language learners. In a great blog post (dating from 2006) he recommends a wide variety of international sites offering free access to resources and apps. There are lots to choose from including Memrise and Duolingo. Please note that FluentU itself is a subscription site.

www.fluentu.com/blog/free-language-learning-websites

10. LOCAL SCHOOLS

If you are a primary colleague and need assistance with language provision, you could approach the languages department at a local secondary to see if they have 'language experts' or 'language prefects'. These are learners who are confident and have excellent languages skills. Aim to forge a link and harness the power of these young people to deliver an hour or an afternoon on vocabulary, phonics or some simple grammar, or to record some short videos. It would be a great experience for them and a free resource for you.

If you are a secondary teacher, encourage your learners to create short teaching videos for Years 5 and 6 using their knowledge and some simple resources. They can plan this as a project, storyboard it, perform it and record their presentation using a digital device. This should be edited by the students, but always verified by you as their teacher. This can then be shared with local primary schools. If your school has its own YouTube channel, the videos can be uploaded and shared with all schools looking for language resources.

There is also another way: designing the curriculum with the learners in mind, setting out from their starting points, guiding and supporting their learning journeys, and expecting the highest from all. This is not achieved by teaching to end-of-year exams or terminal Key Stage 4 or 5 assessments. An authentic, robust and purposeful curriculum crafted for all our learners is the way forward, preparing them for life beyond educational institutions. We need our young people to be inclusive, caring and tolerant, to be educated voices who make a positive impact on their locality, country, continent and world. The curriculum should consider what are the most important skills and languages to acquire, and inspire learners to go beyond their current capabilities, harnessing their imagination, creativity, language skills and competencies to prepare them not just for their exams but for life on the international stage.

The world needs global thinkers, problem-solvers, creative specialists, environmental activists and inspirational entrepreneurs who will write new stories and histories to be shared in many languages. It needs new music, poetry, art and literature – visual and aural feasts to travel the globe and beyond, perhaps, in time, to new galaxies, from a child's bedroom via a keyboard or communication device but always through the medium of a language. The awesome power of language and communication, and its impact, must be shared with young people to ensure that language learning remains a prominent feature of the primary, secondary, post-16 and university sectors, encouraging our learners to travel overseas while also welcoming native speakers from other countries to visit, learn, work and share their stories, cultures and traditions. We need this exchange now more than ever, not only in the UK but across the world.

CHAPTER 10
INFORMATION FOR TRAINEES, NQTS AND RQTS

Congratulations – you are on the journey to enjoying the best job in the world. Here are some tips to help you on your way. Good luck and keep going!

- Smile every day, regardless of what anyone else tells you.

- Make sure you look after yourself; you have to because the job is hard work. This means sleep well, eat well and always have emergency snacks!

- Organise yourself and keep your desk, classroom, teacher planner, bag and space organised too.

- Manage your time well or it will manage you.

- Decide how you want to use your classroom. Place desks as you want them but always make sure the learners are facing you – no backs to the teacher.

- Allocate a clearly labelled box or space for each class to place their exercise books into when you want to collect them in.

- Your teacher planner is worth its weight in gold. Use it – don't lose it.

- Colour code your timetable and have multiple copies of it to hand (on your planner, on your phone, on your desk, in your bag, in your glove box, in your workspace at home).

- Have copies of textbooks and resources at home, and bookmark links to websites on your home computer too – you never know when you might need them.

- Keep your school ID pass (if your school has them), keys and lanyard with you at all times, and put them in your bag at the end of the school day.

- Make sure you have a mentor or buddy (someone from another department who is there to support you), and know who and where the other NQTs are.

- Find time to connect with your buddy – get out of your classroom and have lunch with them.

- Have you joined a teaching union? If not, you need to. Make this a priority.

- Read any information that other teachers have given you, but make up your own mind about your classes. You are a fresh start for these learners.

- Prepare yourself by using class lists and information to create seating plans. Once you know the class you can mix it up to keep them on their toes.

- Make sure you have a scheduled weekly meeting with your head of department or in-school mentor. If anything comes up during the week, make a note of it and bring it up at the meeting. If it needs to be resolved urgently, don't wait to act.

- Attend the sessions with your professional development mentor in school.

- Meet, greet and smile at each class as you welcome them into your learning space.

- Have a settler or pre-starter activity ready for learners to get them thinking and doing as soon as they enter the room.

- Establish clear routines with every class and be consistent. You might want to discuss these with the class, but always be aware of school policies and departmental expectations (ask your head of department for the low-down).

- Use the resources provided by your department but differentiate and develop them so they are accessible for your learners.

- Don't be afraid of being creative – learners love this, and you will too.

- Be brave in the classroom and try out new things. It might take a while to introduce if the learners aren't used to it, but if you are clear and methodical it will enrich your classroom practice.

- Don't pay for online subscriptions from your own pocket. Speak to your department and see what subscriptions are available in school.

- Don't pay for any resources – save the money and use it to treat yourself.

- If you must pay for resources, hold out for sales, search for promotional codes or ask for a discount.

- Stay connected to your friends, university lecturers, personal tutors, university subject specialists, family and special people who make you smile.

- Get connected with other MFL practitioners on Twitter, Facebook languages groups, Instagram and Pinterest. Make sure you protect yourself online – for example, don't use your full name. Check your union and school policies for more on this.

- Build relationships with learners by setting your expectations high; be clear and consistent on this.

- Treat learners with unconditional positive regard. Respect them as individuals and do the best job you can with and for every learner.

- If you have a TA, get to know them and how they work. Make a note of when they are in your lessons and who they will be supporting.

- Always be polite and courteous to other colleagues but most definitely the admin team, the reprographics team, the site team, the cleaners, the exams officer and the ICT team, and always say thank you. These people are the backbone of the school and keep it going.

- Don't tell learners how hard a task is going to be. Although it might motivate some, it may cause others to switch off.

- Don't hold grudges over behaviour-related issues. Speak to the student respectfully (with support if necessary) to establish what the issue is, then draw a line underneath it and carry on as normal.

- If you issue exercise books, be clear on how you expect them to be used in your lessons and at home. Use the back page and back cover to create a pocket for storing important items or ongoing tasks. This will save time throughout the year and you will be grateful for it.

- If you have display space, use it to share and celebrate learners' achievements.

- Don't be afraid to speak with your mentor or buddy or to contact home to find out if there are any issues you need to be aware of or to raise concerns. Double-check the student's name before you do, and keep the communication upbeat and positive.

- When you make a phone call home regarding issues or concerns, ask your buddy or mentor to be present.

- Communicate learners' successes too: parents love a positive phone call home, as do students.

- Have a spare pot of stationery and a pile of paper for learners to use so they can always access the learning without fuss.

- Remember that while being an MFL teacher is hard work, you should always make sure that your learners work harder than you do when in your classroom.

- When reflecting on your lessons, think about what it would be like to be a student in your classroom.

- When planning lessons, consider where you want your learners to be at the end of the lesson and how you will get them there – but always have a plan B, C and D.

- No matter how tired and busy you are, take a moment to reflect on your day. Find three positives and make a note of these in your planner.

- Remember that no one is perfect; we all make mistakes. Aim high, but not for perfection and not at the cost of your health.

- Don't give up! The profession, the learners and the school need you. Ask for help if you are struggling – it will be there in abundance. But no one is a mind reader, so you have to speak up.

- Never be afraid to ask – no question is a stupid question. Any queries you have can be answered by a colleague, the head of department or your buddy. Don't hold on to it and let it keep you awake at night.

- Enjoy yourself!

CHAPTER 11

MFL AND THE WIDER WORLD

The MFL world is rich with subject associations and passionate practitioners who can provide guidance, support, inspiration and a listening ear for languages teachers, when and if they need it. There are also opportunities for collaboration, innovation, development and exchange. The following list is not exhaustive, but it does include some websites, associations and applications which you might not have discovered but are most definitely worth a look.

ASSOCIATIONS

ASSOCIATION FOR LANGUAGE LEARNING

The Association for Language Learning (ALL) is an MFL-focused association. It seeks to raise the profile of the language agenda with government, business and industry, as well as with teachers and practitioners in schools and universities through active participation at a range of events. It is an extremely hardworking group, all of whom are volunteers. The association's densely populated website, magazines and research journals share language practice, expertise and research findings. There is an annual fee to subscribe, but this allows full access to the website (although there are also some free elements).

With over 60 local ALL groups across England and Wales, there are many regional and national face-to-face events, such as Language World, TeachMeets, show and tells, exam-specific sessions and webinars, details of which can be found on the website and on Eventbrite.

www.all-languages.org.uk

@ALL4language

CHARTERED COLLEGE OF TEACHING

The Chartered College of Teaching (CCT) is a membership association which aims to support teachers in working with the latest research and evidence about teaching, learning and pedagogy. Annual membership enables access to online content, such as the journal *Impact,* as well as an extensive research library. Members can access webinars for a small fee, although some are free. Details are emailed to members and shared via Twitter and Eventbrite. The CCT also hosts #CCTLangs on Twitter (led by Dan McPherson (@Dan_MacPherson1)).

www.chartered.college

@CharteredColl

SCOTLAND'S NATIONAL CENTRE FOR LANGUAGES

Scotland's National Centre for Languages (SCILT) provides support for all languages from primary through to senior phase, and is instrumental in placing language learning in the hearts and minds of learners in Scotland. There is lots of support for languages promotion, teaching and learning through the 1+2 approach (the Scottish government's aspiration that by 2021 every child will learn their first additional language in primary 1 and a second in primary 5), as well as access to language research papers and documents. SCILT also provides information for young people at different stages of their language learning journey.

www.scilt.org.uk

@scottishcilt

LANGUAGES FOR EDUCATION EUROPE

Based in Edinburgh and delivering CPD and support to teachers across Europe, Languages for Education Europe (LFEE) focuses on the teaching and learning of French, Spanish and English in primary and secondary schools for teachers at all stages of their careers.

www.lfee.net

@LfeeEurope

SOCIAL MEDIA

FACEBOOK

There is much support available on Facebook for linguists through a range of discussion groups – for example:

- ELAPSE
- Global Innovative Language Teachers (GILT)
- iGCSE Language Teachers
- Language Matters
- Languages in Primary Schools (LIPS)

- Light Bulb Languages

- MFL 9–1 Resources

- MFL Fun

- MFL Matters

- MFL Middle Leadership Matters

- MFL TeachMeets

- MFL Wales

- New GCSE MFL

- Polly Glot Languages

- Primary Languages

- Primary Languages Network

- Secondary MFL in Wales

- Secondary MFL Matters

- Vale Languages

A Facebook account is required to access the groups, some of which are closed so permission needs to be granted in order to join. You will also need to abide by the code of conduct. Some brilliant professional communities are available within Facebook groups, so they are definitely worth investigating and joining. The groups support fellow teachers and share resources, tips and advice.

TWITTER AND #MFLTWITTERATI

Joe Dale (@joedale) is well known for sharing his diverse knowledge about supporting and training MFL teachers. He started #MFLTwitterati, which teachers, trainees, school leaders, learning support assistants and FLAs use to come together to help, share and support one another through the trials, tribulations, celebrations and joys of being an MFL practitioner. If you aren't already a member, do get involved – it's free to join. You can use the MFLTwitterati hashtag to share languages tweets, ideas and questions, and to connect with thousands of other language practitioners. Joe has also started an MFLTwitterati podcast, which might be of interest.

https://mfltwitteratipodcast.com/about/

PINTEREST

Pinterest is an amazing platform for sharing and collecting ideas and visuals to use in the classroom as resources or for display, from collections of realia to interesting posters. It's free to join, and easy to search for, collect and share the images on your pinboards.

www.pinterest.co.uk

ORGANISATIONS

BRITISH COUNCIL

The British Council have sites across the globe to promote all things British and the learning of English as an additional language. As well as promoting cultural exchange to support the teaching and learning of English overseas, the British Council also promote Wales, Scotland and Ireland.

www.britishcouncil.org

www.britishcouncil.ie

https://scotland.britishcouncil.org

https://wales.britishcouncil.org

The British Council's International School Award recognises and rewards schools that have shown a commitment to embedding internationalism and raising awareness and understanding across the school community. An international project, an element of the curriculum or school values which impact the school community, families and the wider community can all qualify schools for this prestigious award.

www.britishcouncil.org/school-resources/accreditation/international-school-award

Connecting Classrooms is a scheme supported by the British Council which connects UK classrooms with other classrooms across the world to assist in the development of language skills and the knowledge and understanding of different cultures, thereby promoting communication and tolerance. It is highly beneficial to learners in terms of widening horizons as well as opening hearts to different experiences and lifestyles through shared projects, education and global learning.

https://connecting-classrooms.britishcouncil.org

eTwinning is responsible for over 80,000 twinning projects, connecting teachers, educators and learners in European and some neighbouring countries. Joint online projects can be constructed and supported for children aged from 3 to 19 to enrich learning, understanding and skills. There are lots of online resources and project ideas to support global learning. eTwinning can also support International School Award applications. This scheme may be affected by the UK's decision to leave the European Union.

www.britishcouncil.org/etwinning

ERASMUS+

Erasmus+ offers a range of incredible opportunities for sixth formers, apprentices and university students to study, work, volunteer, teach or train across Europe, helping them to gain invaluable experience and develop a range of skills, thereby improving their expertise and employability. There are also opportunities for teachers, trainees and FLAs. Erasmus+ may be affected by the UK's departure from the European Union.

www.erasmusplus.org.uk

GOETHE-INSTITUT

The Goethe-Institut is Germany's official cultural institute, providing advice, support and resources for teaching the German language, but also for German literature, film, music, and social and political history through cultural events and exchanges. Language courses are available for learners, and support, training and resources are available for teachers, leaders and FLAs, either face to face or online.

www.goethe.de/ins/gb/en/ueb.html

INSTITUT FRANÇAIS

Institut Français is part of a worldwide network which promotes the French language and culture as well as promoting cross-cultural exchange and diversity. Institut Français supports teachers, trainees and FLAs to develop a rich and varied cultural curriculum through the medium of the French language. It provides face-to-face and online lessons, in addition to events such as French film programmes.

www.institut-francais.org.uk

INSTITUTO CERVANTES

Instituto Cervantes is an official Spanish language and cultural centre, with bases in 80 countries across the globe to provide teachers, students and learners with support and information about the Spanish language, and culture and literature from Spain and Latin America. Instituto Cervantes also provides professional support and training for teachers, including face-to-face and online development, and Spanish lessons.

www.londres.cervantes.es

MUNDOLINGUA

The Museum of Languages is a fantastic little museum near le Jardin du Luxembourg in the 6th arrondissement. This is a must-visit if you find yourself in Paris or are seeking out a new destination for language learners to explore and learn more about language through artefacts, quizzes and games in both analogue and digital formats. On entering you are immersed in thousands of items which language learners and language geeks can explore at their leisure or with assistance on a guided tour. It is perfect for students and teachers, but do get in touch with the museum beforehand if you are with a group. There is so much to see and do, all promoting and exploring a range of languages.

www.mundolingua.org/en

ONLINE RESOURCES

BUSUU

Busuu is a free language learning app which challenges users to learn to speak a language in only ten minutes per day. Although currently there is only a small range of languages to learn, over 90 million users have signed up. You can choose your language starting point and work through lessons, quizzes, vocabulary and phrases to improve your language skills. It is available for Apple and Android devices. Although Busuu offers a free trial, there is a paid subscription to access the full range of services.

www.busuu.com

DUOLINGO

Duolingo is a hit with over 1.2 billion people who have signed up to its free content to learn languages. Duolingo's mission is to create a fun language learning platform that can be accessed across the globe and which provides personalised languages education to anyone who has access to the internet. Online progress tracking has recently been made available to allow languages teachers to assess the impact on students of Duolingo's independent learning tasks.

www.duolingo.com

www.schools.duolingo.com

ELAPSE

This research project aims to develop teachers' under-standing and awareness of CLIL, as well as to build their confidence, skills, knowledge and expertise in order to empower them to introduce CLIL methodology into their planning and lessons. The ELAPSE project will create lesson plans and resources for teachers – in both primary and secondary settings – as well as a good practice guide to support the teaching of French, German, Spanish and English through the CLIL method.

www.lfee.net/category/erasmus-plus-elapse/

https://www.all-languages.org.uk/initiatives/
elapse-embedding-languages-across-primary-and-
secondary-education/

FRENCH TEACHER

French Teacher is a brilliant site created by author and former teacher Steve Smith (@spsmith45) which provides resources to support languages teachers, trainees, FLAs and TAs. There is a subscription fee to access the full range of resources, presentations and exercises. Steve has col-lated a wonderful range of tools and advice that can be used in any French or Spanish language classroom from Year 7 through to A level.

www.frenchteacher.net

KAHOOT!

Kahoot! is a free game-based learning platform aimed at schools and businesses. It can be used to support inter-leaving, spacing and low-stakes testing with groups or individuals, either in class or outside it. Teachers decide on the format and content, and then create a game by adding engaging images, videos or diagrams. Great fun and engaging!

www.kahoot.com

LANGUAGE MAGICIAN

Language Magician is an award-winning game created with languages development and immersive learning in mind. It is great fun for primary age children who develop not only their language skills but also their ICT skills. A positive feature for teachers is a tracking and monitoring facility which shows learners' level of progress through assessments that appear throughout the game. Language Magician is free, although it is necessary to open an account. The game is a unique project which is being supported across four countries by primary language learning experts alongside several universities which are researching the impact of the game on users' language development.

www.thelanguagemagician.net

LANGUAGE GYM

Language Gym, which was created by Dr Gianfranco Conti, contains many resources and support materials designed for maximum impact in the classroom, but also to encourage learners to develop and practise key language skills independently. Language Gym is designed for languages teachers and trainees and covers the full range of language skills, exam skills and preparatory work for French, Spanish and some Italian.

https://www.language-gym.com

https://gianfrancoconti.com

LIGHT BULB LANGUAGES

Light Bulb Languages is a superb free languages resources site created and curated by Clare Seccombe (@valleseco). Covering French, Spanish, German, Italian and Latin from primary to A level, Light Bulb Languages offers a rich collection of resources with ideas for starters and plenaries through to thinking skills and displays. There are also suggestions for schemes of learning which are fully resourced for primary schools, with upskilling podcasts to provide support for busy teachers and language specialists.

www.lightbulblanguages.co.uk

LINGUASCOPE

If you have been teaching for a few years, you will know exactly what I mean when I refer to 'the website with the fish'. Linguascope is a subscription service which enables learners to learn, reinforce and develop their vocabulary through games and repeat recall activities. There are also downloadable worksheets and resources across five languages to reinforce online practice.

www.linguascope.co.uk

MEMRISE

Memrise is a free online learning platform with over 40 million users which enables learners to select and follow a range of courses. From a language perspective, Memrise allows members to create language learning courses which can be shared either with a specific class of learners or with the wider world. It boasts real-life language content, including videos created by native speakers, and fun learning experiences.

www.memrise.com

TEACHIT LANGUAGES

Teachit Languages has developed from Teachit, a resources site to support teachers to find inspiration and tried and tested resources. The subscription site has resources available in French, German and Spanish across Key Stages 3 to 5, from practical cultural resources to grammar quizzes and exam support materials.

www.teachitlanguages.co.uk

THIS IS LANGUAGE

This is Language is a subscription-based online platform which provides an impressive range of authentic language videos in French, German, Spanish and Italian, aimed at secondary to university-level learners. There are over 5,000 videos with a range of themes and levels, plus a selection of rigorous exercises that students can complete to show they have understood the content.

www.thisislanguage.com

VOCAB EXPRESS

Vocab Express is another subscription-based online learning tool which is designed to engage students in learning vocabulary and grammar and to develop their pronunciation skills through gamification. It is highly engaging and there are packages available for schools.

www.vocabexpress.com

RESOURCE LIST

This list includes links to the resources that I have mentioned throughout the book.

PHONICS

Active Phonics

https://activephonics.co.uk

Springwell Special Academy

https://springwelllearningcommunity.co.uk/about-us/active-phonics

Hip Hop Phonics (Nina Elliott)

www.slideserve.com/beulah/hip-hop-phonics

Les Planètes Phoniques, Los Planetas Fonéticos, Die Phonetikplaneten (Wendy Adjenii and Juliet Park)

www.trainingforlearning.co.uk/planetes_phonique.htm

ORACY

School 21

www.school21.org.uk/voice21

Voice 21

www.voice21.org

OTHERS

21 Questions

http://20q.net

Apple Clips

www.apple.com/uk/clips

Brainbox

www.brainbox.co.uk/brainbox-range

Classtools

www.classtools.net

Pose, pause, pounce, bounce

www.youtube.com/watch?v=TMBsTw37eaE

Kloo

https://kloogame.com

Primary Languages Network

https://primarylanguages.network

Sue Cave

www.cavelanguages.co.uk

This is Language

www.thisislanguage.com

Word Clouds

http://www.wordclouds.com

YAKiT Kids

https://yakit-kids-ios.soft112.com

I blog about my classroom practice, adventures in learning and MFL at: https://cristahazell.wordpress.com.

REFERENCES AND FURTHER READING

All-Party Parliamentary Group on Modern Languages (2019) A National Recovery Programme for Languages: A Framework Proposal from the All-Party Parliamentary Group on Modern Languages (4 March). Available at: https://secure.toolkitfiles.co.uk/clients/34124/sitedata/files/A-national-recovery-programme-for-languages.pdf.

Bauckham, I. (2016) *Modern Foreign Languages Pedagogy Review: A Review of Modern Foreign Languages Teaching Practice in Key Stage 3 and Key Stage 4* (Teaching Schools Council). Available at: https://pure.york.ac.uk/portal/files/54043904/MFL_Pedagogy_Review_Report_TSC_PUBLISHED_VERSION_Nov_2016_1_.pdf.

Beere, J. (2020) *Independent Thinking on Teaching and Learning: Developing Independence and Resilience in All Teachers and Learners* (Carmarthen: Independent Thinking Press).

Benson, J. (2016) The Power of Positive Regard, *Educational Leadership* 73: 22–26. Available at: http://www.ascd.org/publications/educational-leadership/jun16/vol73/num09/The-Power-of-Positive-Regard.aspx.

Berger, R. (2012) *Critique and Feedback: The Story of Austin's Butterfly* (8 December) [video]. Available at: https://www.youtube.com/watch?v=hqh1MRWZjms.

Clark, C. and Teravainen, A. (2017) Celebrating Reading for Enjoyment: Findings from our Annual Literacy Survey 2016 (London: National Literacy Trust). Available at: https://literacytrust.org.uk/research-services/research-reports/celebrating-reading-enjoyment-findings-our-annual-literacy-survey-2016-report.

Clowes, G. (2011) The Essential 5: A Starting Point for Kagan Cooperative Lerning, *Kagan Online Magazine* (San Clemente, CA: Kagan Publishing). Available at: https://kaganonline.com/free_articles/research_and_rationale/330/The-Essential-5-A-Starting-Point-for-Kagan-Cooperative-Learning.

Department for Education (2013) *Languages Programmes of Study: Key Stage 2 National Curriculum in England* (September). Ref: DFE-00174-2013. Available at: https://assets.publishing.service. gov.uk/government/uploads/system/uploads/attachment_data/ file/239042/PRIMARY_national_curriculum_-_Languages.pdf.

Department for Education (2014) *Promoting Fundamental British Values as Part of SMSC on Schools: Departmental Advice for Maintained Schools* (27 November). Ref: DFE-00679-2014. Available at: https://www.gov.uk/government/publications/ promoting-fundamental-british-values-through-smsc.

Department for Education and Department of Health and Social Care (2015) *Special Educational Needs and Disability Code of Practice: 0 to 25 Years* (January). Ref: DFE-00205-2013. Available at: https://www.gov.uk/government/publications/send-code-of- practice-0-to-25.

Expert Subject Advisory Group – Modern Foreign Languages (2015) *Assessment in Modern Foreign Languages in the Primary School* (January). Available at: https://www.all-languages.org.uk/ wp-content/uploads/2016/01/ESAGMFLGroupAssessment- Statement.pdf.

Gilbert, I. (2007) *The Little Book of Thunks: 260 Questions to Make Your Brain Go Ouch!* (Carmarthen: Independent Thinking Press).

Grosjean, F. (2011) Change of Language, Change of Personality?, *Psychology Today* (1 November). Available at: https://www. psychologytoday.com/gb/blog/life-bilingual/201111/change-language- change-personality.

Halliday, J. (2018) 'We Batter Them with Kindness': Schools That Reject Super-Strict Values, *The Guardian* (27 February). Available at: https://www.theguardian.com/education/2018/feb/27/ schools-discipline-unconditional-positive-regard.

Holmes, B. and Myles, F. (2019) *White Paper: Primary Languages Policy in England – The Way Forward* (Research in Primary Languages). Available at: http://www.ripl.uk/wp-content/uploads/ 2019/02/RIPL-White-Paper-Primary-Languages-Policy-in- England.pdf.

House of Commons Library (2019) Language Teaching in Schools (England). Briefing Paper 07388 (16 October). Available at: https://

researchbriefings.parliament.uk/ResearchBriefing/Summary/
CBP-7388.

Kagan, S. and Kagan, M. (2009) *Kagan Cooperative Learning* (San Clemente, CA: Kagan Publishing).

Kelley, T. and Kelley, D. (2014) Resource: 30 Circles – Creativity Challenge, *UKEdChat* (27 May). Available at: https://ukedchat.com/2014/05/27/resource-30-circles-creativity-challenge.

Kerka, S. (2000) Incidental Learning: Trends and Issues Alert No. 18. Available at: https://files.eric.ed.gov/fulltext/ED446234.pdf.

Luna, D., Ringberg, T. and Peracchio, L. A. (2008) One Individual, Two Identities: Frame Switching among Biculturals, *Journal of Consumer Research* 35(2): 279–293. Available at: https://www.researchgate.net/publication/23547452_One_Individual_Two_Identities_Frame_Switching_among_Biculturals.

Ofsted (2018) *Working Together to Safeguard Children: A Guide to Inter-agency Working to Safeguard and Promote the Welfare of Children* (July). Ref: DFE-00195-2018. Available at: https://www.gov.uk/government/publications/working-together-to-safeguard-children--2.

Prentis, N. (2017) Feel More Fun in French? Your Personality Can Change Depending on the Language You Speak, *Quartz* (8 March). Available at: https://qz.com/925630/feel-more-fun-in-french-your-personality-can-change-depending-on-the-language-you-speak.

Mahmoudzadeh, M., Dehaene-Lambertz, G., Fournier, M., Kongolo, G., Goudjil, S., Dubois, J., Grebe, R. and Wallois, F. (2013) Syllabic Discrimination in Premature Human Infants Prior to Complete Formation of Cortical Layers, *Proceedings of the National Academy of Sciences of the United States of America* 110(12): 4846–4851. Available at: https://www.pnas.org/content/110/12/4846.

Mishan, F. (2005) *Designing Authenticity into Language Learning Materials* (Bristol: Intellect).

Myers, H. (2013) French: Avoir, to Have – Present Tense (10 February) [video]. Available at: https://www.youtube.com/watch?v=3kWwS1_Kark.

Roberts, M. (2013) Babies Can Hear Syllables in the Womb, Says Research, *BBC News* (26 February). Available at: https://www.bbc.co.uk/news/health-21572520.

Seccombe, C. (2013) Make It with Mini-Books, *Changing Phase* (22 March) [blog]. Available at: http://changing-phase.blogspot.com/2013/03/make-it-with-mini-books.html.

Solak, E. (2016) Teaching Listening Skills. In E. Solak (ed.), *Teaching Language Skills for Prospective English Teachers* (Istanbul: Pelikan), pp. 29–44.

Tinsley, T. (2019) *Language Trends 2019: Language Teaching in Primary and Secondary Schools in England. Survey Report* (London: British Council). Available at: https://www.britishcouncil.org/research-policy-insight/research-reports/language-trends-2019.

Tinsley, T. and Board, K. (2013) *Languages for the Future: Which Languages the UK Needs Most and Why* (London: British Council). Available at: https://www.britishcouncil.org/sites/default/files/languages-for-the-future-report.pdf.

Tinsley, T. and Board, K. (2017) *Languages for the Future: The Foreign Languages the United Kingdom Needs to Become a Truly Global Nation* (London: British Council). Available at: https://www.britishcouncil.org/sites/default/files/languages_for_the_future_2017.pdf.

Tinsley, T. and Doležal, N. (2018) *Language Trends 2018: Language Teaching in Primary and Secondary Schools in England. Survey Report* (London: British Council). Available at: https://www.britishcouncil.org/sites/default/files/language_trends_2018_report.pdf.

Vanderplank, R. (2014) Listening and Understanding. In P. Driscoll, E. Macaro and A. Swarbrick (eds), *Debates in Modern Languages Education* (Abingdon and New York: Routledge), pp. 53–65.

Webb, H. (2019) Revision Techniques: Interleaving and Spacing, *SecEd* (3 April). Available at: http://www.sec-ed.co.uk/best-practice/revision-techniques-interleaving-and-spacing/.

Wiliam, D. (2016) PPPB – Pose, Pause, Pounce, Bounce [video] (8 September). Available at: https://www.youtube.com/watch?v=TMBsTw37eaE.

978-178135337-0

978-178135338-7

978-178135339-4

978-178135340-0

978-178135341-7

978-178135353-0

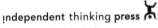

independent thinking press
www.independentthinkingpress.com

independent thinking

Independent Thinking. An education company.

Taking people's brains for a walk since 1994.

We use our words.

www.independentthinking.com